MINDFULNESS FOR ANXIETY

HOW TO OVERCOME ANXIETY AND DEPRESSION, RELIEVE STRESS, STOP WORRYING, ELIMINATE NEGATIVE THINKING, AND RETURN TO A STATE OF PEACE AND HAPPINESS.

By Roberta Rivera

Table of Contents

Introduction

As was mentioned in the introduction, a journey toward mindfulness begins from within. Inner peace is a thing we hear about often, but may feel is outside of our reach. Many people talk about it, and seek it out, never knowing that the search itself may be the very thing that is keeping them from attaining it. Trying so hard to control the external world in an effort to gain inner peace seems to be a common method, yet it is counterproductive and only creates more turmoil. The first step to inner peace is letting go. There are several other elements to help one obtain peacefulness, but letting go is foremost. Creating inner peace is mostly an understanding between yourself and the world that you are who you are, and the world is not in control. Everything that occurs outside of you only interferes with your inner peace when you allow it to by reacting to it.

That's right; you control your inner peace with how you react to the things that happen in your life and in the world around you. In this very important , we will address this, and work on the things you can do that will help you have a better grasp on inner peace.

Let's begin with old business. Although the focus in this is introspection, one cannot leave things unresolved from a time when inner peace was not a priority. Things from the past that may still be a source of turmoil for you must be put to rest. Having things unfinished will feel that way until you finish them. They will continue to interfere in your journey to mindfulness and need to be resolved.

Apologize to whomever you know you should. Make amends with whomever you can, even if it's only for the sake of your inner peace. Tie up the loose ends that you may have left at schools, old workplaces, old living situations, and any other relationship of any kind. Most importantly, forgive everyone. Once you have forgiven, you take away any power those issues have over you. It is empowering and freeing to let them know you have forgiven them, in any way you are able. It helps everyone involved, and you can mark that off your list forever. Resolve each of the open-ended contentions, and settle up all of your affairs. This will ease you into acceptance.

Letting things go will become easier the more you do it, and you have already practiced surrender and acceptance by resolving lingering matters. Now you can take it a step further by deciding to completely accept all things that you cannot change, and surrendering to what is. This does not mean to throw your hands up in the air and give up. There is a finesse required to keep from crossing the line between accepting and just checking out. Acknowledgement is the key to acceptance. You must first let yourself be aware of the things you cannot change in order to surrender and truly accept them. An example of this could be spilled milk. You can ignore it, and decide not to let it affect you, but it eventually will by becoming a rotten, stinky mess. When you notice the spilled milk, accept that it was spilled, and surrender to the fact that you must clean it up and move on; you eliminate spilled milk disrupting your peace and keep yourself from a more difficult and odious problem in the future.

This leads us to the next element of finding inner peace, and it's a biggie. Choose your own behavior, and take responsibility for your actions and reactions to the world. Decide who you want to be, and put forth an effort to maintain your inner peace in any possible situation. Other people, places, and events do not make you behave any particular way. You are not a puppet. You are in control and are ultimately responsible for how you express yourself. Decide to take full responsibility for your reactions to the world around you. It's important to trust yourself with the information given to you, solicited or not, and slow your reaction time so as to decide how you would like to react, or whether to react at all. Self-control is a very big part of choosing your own behavior, and practicing it will make it easier to give yourself the time to remember who you have chosen to be and make a choice in how you respond.

Of course, this does not mean you are a perfect stoic tower of tranquility at all times. Taking responsibility for your actions and reactions means that no matter what your response is, you claim your part in it. None of us is perfect, even people on the journey to mindfulness. When the outside world does its thing, we will sometimes receive that information, forget to take the time to remember for ourselves who we want to be in every situation, and human nature takes over to produce a reaction from us that we may not be proud of. That's ok. We must accept it, take responsibility for it, and address the feelings that may have gotten us to that place.

Addressing the feelings you have will lead you to become perceptive and aware of all feelings, yours as well as those of others. Figure out what pushes your buttons, and try to understand why those things are triggers for you. Hard to face, and otherwise uncomfortable feelings come with a message, and it is important to your inner peace that you acknowledge and attempt to understand them. A good way to do this is to metaphorically hold the emotion in your hands, and examine it. Ask yourself where this feeling might be coming from. Why do you think you are feeling this? Is there an underlying cause? Take note of whatever you discover, allow yourself to feel that feeling, accept it, and let it go.

Once you've learned to be more aware of feelings, you can work on honesty, with yourself and others. Telling the truth is a very important part of attaining inner peace for several reasons. For one, it keeps your mind free. There are no lies to remember as well as no guilt weighing you down. Another reason honesty is important is because if you aren't being truthful with yourself about things you need to let go, those things won't hold any meaning if you've sabotaged the process by altering what the real focus needs to be. Lastly, being truthful will assist in your journey to inner peace by allowing you to say what you really feel and think. It is very liberating to genuinely express yourself, and your world becomes a lot more simplified when you aren't constantly juggling how your feelings may affect others while attempting to anticipate their reaction to them. Learn ways to tell the truth while still being kind. Your integrity will take you much further than the instant gratification a lie provides.

Integrity will be a positive side effect of your inner peace, and knowing your higher self comes along with it. When you get to the emotions behind the reasons for your reactions to your external environment, it will ultimately bring you to ego, and lower consciousness. Just by recognizing this, you are living as your higher self. We all have ego, and we all have to work with it, but taking the time to examine ourselves and learn about the driving force behind how we interact with the world puts us on the path to inner peace. Distinguish between your true self versus the outward personality you share with the world. Most likely, the person you show to the world is a combination of ego, your surface level needs, and past experiences. Take the time to explore the person you really are, and begin to let your veritable self come forth. What are your values and ideals? What brings you joy? What are you passionate about? The answers to those questions are what define you; this is your authentic self.

The detachment from your false self and keeping your ego in check will go more smoothly if you begin to slow down. There is no place for overworking, winning, outdoing, or competing when mindfulness is the goal. Move more slowly, take the time needed to complete tasks, and make an effort to not feel rushed. Everything we do takes time, and giving yourself time to do things in a deliberate manner means that you are more peaceful while moving through your day. Give up the fight, and sit it out while you gain invaluable inner peace.

Slowing down may cause you to begin to notice small imbalances in your life that had previously been overlooked. It is important that you give these matters some focus, and address them as needed. They are your opportunities to practice what you have learned. When you sense a disharmony, acknowledge that you cannot change everything, examine the discord, separate yourself from it, and address it in a healthy way. You will become more sensitive to damaging influences, and get better at handling them with a sense of mindful tranquility.

When you make inner peace the priority, your focus becomes clear. Implementing the skills you now have can bring you to a place of inner peace more quickly and easily the more you make it commonplace. Your inner peace will become a predominant fixture in your everyday life once you decide for yourself that it is.

Chapter 1 What is Mindfulness?

Before jumping into dissecting how mindfulness can help you, it is important to take a step back and actually understand what mindfulness is. I mean, you've probably heard of it a lot, but do you actually know what it is? If you don't know what it is, how can you expect to know you've attained it?

A more interesting question to ponder over is whether mindfulness is something that can even be attained. In Western culture, we've structured our lives around the chasing of goals and objectives. A life without a goal is a pointless existence, so we've been told. Everyone needs to have a defined ambition and things aren't given to you, you have to go out and grab them.

This is true of material things and the stuff you don't have but how can you grab at something you already have? This is the conundrum about mindfulness; most people in our society fail to understand. You see, you already have the ability to be mindful. You just need to allow it.

Brain Surgery

Mindfulness as a practice finds its origins in ancient Buddhist principles but its versatility is such that it has been adopted by a wide variety of religions since. Indeed, all of the major religions of this world have devoted to being mindful and being present in every task that we do.

Presence is what is central to mindfulness. By being present you're acknowledging the only instant in time you have available to you. However, mindfulness goes beyond just being present. The true crux of the practice is observation. Adopting a third person's viewpoint of your thoughts and actions is what all mindfulness boils down to.

So, if you think about it, what you're doing is analyzing your own brain. This is why mindfulness is so difficult to practice. It's easy to think that you can be present and focus completely on what you're doing right now but reality offers a different experience. Try focusing on your breath this instant. Notice how you inhale and exhale and try to explore the quality of your breath.

Notice whether it's hot or cold. Where does it hit your skin on exhalation? Can you feel where it goes when you inhale? Now, think back to what your mind was doing as you were observing your breath. Odds are that it was focused on something else or that it was bringing up weird images in your mind.

Then there are those people who claim to be fully focused. There are only two groups of people who experience this state. The first are the truly enlightened and they are unlikely to be reading this book. The second are the rank beginners. This is because such people are not even aware of what their mind is doing.

I'm not mentioning this to make you feel bad. It's just a fact. The good news is that you're going to learn exactly how much of a chatterbox your mind can be and why ignoring it for the most part is one of the best things you'll do in your life.

Greater Understanding

Buddhist philosophy views mindfulness as being the path one needs to take in order to understand the truth about the universe. There's a lot of moving parts to that statement, so let's break it down a bit. First is the detail regarding mindfulness being a path. You see, practicing mindfulness isn't just about doing a few exercises, as I've mentioned before, it's about living a certain way.

As you live mindfully, you'll learn more about yourself and how your mind reacts. When you keep progressing along this path, at some point, you'll realize that you can observe the same delusions you operate under in others around you. You'll begin to detect that point in time where your brain or the other person's brain chooses to react to the sensory stimulus they receive.

You'll notice that between the moment when something happens to you and the moment when you decide to react to it, there exists a gap. The gap is the most peaceful state of being and true presence is found here. It will be a fleeting thing and you will chase it. Once you chase it enough, you'll realize that it has always been there, and you need to allow it to exist instead of running after an image of it.

This is just a small taste of the path that will unfold before you. Everyone experiences things differently and this is why mindfulness isn't a path of understanding the world as much as it is all about figuring out who you are. Is there even a difference between understanding yourself and the universe? You'll find out!

This brings us to the next portion of our initial sentence which talks about "understanding." What is understanding and what is knowledge? Often the two are confused for one another. Who is better equipped to deal with the world, a person who has excellent interpersonal skills or a recluse genius mathematician? Obviously, it's the former. But who's understands things better?

Who has a better grasp of reality? This opens another line of thought. What is reality? The journey you will undertake will bring about all sorts of questions like these. It is easy and very pleasing to our ego to sit around and pontificate about all of these things, but the fact is that all of our opinions about these things are worth as much as piece of garbage in the overall scheme of things.

Doing and practicing is what counts when it comes to mindfulness and without practice, you cannot hope to acquire any knowledge. The true nature of knowledge is thus the journey itself and not the destination. Along the way, as you observe what triggers you, you'll gain a deeper insight into what the nature of your reality is and how you have created it.

Reality is created by your intention. Intention is a nebulous thing and cannot be described with any great accuracy. Intention can be best thought of as the spirit with which you live your life. Ancient Buddhism opines that by fixing the right intention, a person's journey in life becomes that much easier. What is the right intention? Briefly, it is to practice right action and right thought.

What is right action and thought? Well, at this point we'd be going deep into Buddhist philosophy and that is not the point of this book. The aim is to apply mindfulness to achieve improvements in your life, namely by reducing the amount of stress you experience. So, let's just say that your actions and intentions need to be aligned on achieving a more harmonious view with the world.

This means you need to align yourself with the reality that is around you. The more your reality conflicts with what is around you, universal reality so to speak, the greater the stress and disconnect you will experience. You expect things to go left but the world goes right. You undertake stress.

You think you're qualified for the job, but your boss doesn't and promotes someone else instead. Stress. The world is loaded with all kinds of stress triggers for us and the mistake we make is that we try to change the world. If a loved one behaves a certain way, that annoys us, what is our typical reaction? Well, if you're like most people, you probably tell them to cut it out. You try to get them to stop.

Mindfulness will get you to realize that you cannot control things which are outside of you. The more you try to control them, the more out of sync with reality you become and the more the suffering you heap on yourself. In this context, suffering can be thought of as being stressed.

Think back to what happens when you keep telling your loved one to change their behavior. One day they simply refuse, and this results in a dramatic fight. Good luck not getting stressed out from that! True wisdom recognizes that change only comes from within since this is the only aspect of your life you fully control. Everything else is out of your hands and you have no business worrying about or trying to control any of that.

Progression

So, your intention is fixed to trying to align yourself to the world and to reduce the disconnect between inside and outside. What happens now? Well, once your intention changes you begin expressing this with your thoughts and words. These are what create your reality and are how people form impressions of you.

Really what's happening is that your intention is what creates your environment. The environment we surround ourselves with is extremely important.

Research has shown that we mimic the actions and behavior of the people closest to us (ANTONOPOULOS, 2016). Everything from money, success and behavior is molded by your environment, whether when you were a child or an adult.

A lot of people try to change the outside world, again, by trying to force their worldview on their environment, that is, the people around them. Some even succeed for a while but this is the wrong way to go about things. Trying to control the thoughts and the will of others is a futile task and when it does blow up, it's pretty spectacular. Think back to how any dictator or despot has received their comeuppance.

Here, again, we see that the thing to do is to change your intention and allow this to change your environment. The actions you need to take are very little in this case. After all, you only need to seek to align yourself with where you want to be in your life. One of the biggest causes of stress is the fact that people are in one place and they want to be in another.

They might say their intention is to be elsewhere, but intention is betrayed by action. If a person continues to behave in the old manner or doesn't seem to be making any effort with regards to changing their situation, you can safely assume their intention is exactly where they are right now.

What you think and say is what creates actions and how you act is how you'll behave. Your behavior is the sum of everything you want and currently believe. There is usually a disconnect when it comes to our beliefs and our intention. This isn't as big of a deal as it sounds. I mean to say that if you're in one place and want to get to another, it is obvious you're going to have to learn new things to get there.

Your belief system is shaped by your environment and thus, if you set your intention right, the environment you need will be created by you and this will have an effect on your beliefs. Your beliefs in turn will further shape your environment and thus the feedback loop goes on and on.

It is in your interest to create a virtuous feedback loop instead of a vicious one as you can imagine. Your behavior will eventually come to define who you are in the eyes of the world. The sum of your behavior in various situations is what is called character. Character is what draws people and positive situations into your life and is what people ultimately see when they look at one another.

It is easy to adopt someone's character when looking to model a successful outcome, but the fact is that you need to dig deeper and figure out what their intention is. Intention is what guides everything and is the root of your existence. Fix your intention to be mindful and present and you'll create an environment which supports this, bit by bit.

Thought Patterns

Mindfulness will illuminate your thought patterns, as I've mentioned. By observing your mind, you'll be assuming the role of the impartial observer, not judging or questioning anything, but just observing. It sounds easy to do but the reality is a lot different. After all, you're the one you're observing, and it is hard to do this without making things personal.

If you're careening towards disaster, should you remain impersonal? No one can. The issue is that almost everything can seem like a disaster and the process of figuring out what is a big deal and what isn't is a lot like having a bandage ripped off on an unhealed wound. It hurts.

Mindfulness isn't a passive process. It requires you to sit there and take stock of things and remain steadfast on your path. If anything, it is the most active process out there because this is how you engage in life and create a reality for yourself. There are two ways of practicing mindfulness, formal and informal.

The formal method is what monks do, which is to say that they dedicate their lives to the practice and spend long stretches of the day in meditation. Every action of theirs is informed by spiritual prescription. The informal method is to bring mindfulness to everyday actions. For example, if you're eating, becoming mindful of what you're eating and of being fully present without distraction is practicing informal mindfulness.

Personally, I find a mixture of both is the best way forward. This establishes a mindset of continuous practice and improvement. Set aside some time every day to conduct a formal practice but also keep practicing as you go about your day to the best of your abilities. Remember, if you set your intention to be mindful, you will create an environment which will encourage you to practice mindfulness.

Let's look at an example of mindful practice. Since I've mentioned eating something, we might as well begin with this. Let's say you're eating almonds and want to be more mindful of it. Pick up a single almond and begin:

The aim is to explore the almond with all of your senses. This is what it means to be aware of something. Set your intention as such. Act as if you've never seen it before (and you probably never truly have).

Run your fingers over the ridges and feel how coarse it is. Does the coarseness vary depending on the region of the almond? How do the edges feel? Do they pierce your fingers?

What is the shape of the solitary nut like? Keep running your fingers to understand it and feel the texture. It feels rough for sure. What about the temperature of the skin? Is it hot, cold, room temperature? As you press onto the almond can you feel your pulse in your fingertips?

How does it feel in the palm of your hand? It feels small, doesn't it? Roll it around a little between your fingers and notice how different fingers react to it. As you switch fingers can you feel the new sense of touch running from your fingers to the inside your body via your nerves?

Now, smell it. Does it have a smell at all? What does it remind you of, if it does?

Think about wanting to eat the almond. Notice how the minute you think about it, your arm automatically moves and brings it closer to your mouth. Now, open your mouth and place it on your tongue without chewing it.

Roll it around inside and notice how your mouth becomes wet with saliva. This happens automatically and you didn't have to do anything to generate it. You didn't even think about it. Notice how your body is like a machine that just does things on autopilot.

As you're rolling it inside your mouth, think back to the thoughts that have been running through your head since the first step. What have they been? What words have they contained? Notice your reactions to those words. Don't judge, just notice and let them go. Once this is done, get back to your almond.

Bite it and begin to chew it. The texture feels a lot different. Notice the sound that is generated when you chew. What does your tongue feel like when the almond's insides hits your taste buds?

Swallow the almond and feel it pass down your throat. Notice any other internal sensations as this happens.

This exercise is just a taste of what mindfulness is all about. I'd like to note that you don't need to consciously think in this manner each and every time you do these things. Once you set your intention to be mindful, your body will follow, and you will begin to notice these things all by yourself.

As you do this, notice the number of things that are going on within you and around you. Do you realize how much of your world you simply take for granted? Think of all the things happening within your body right now. That solitary almond is contributing to this machine that is in your possession. How cool is that!

You see, this is what mindfulness does. It awakens you to things you cannot see with your eyes. Now that you've got a taste of mindfulness, let's move forward and establish a base for your mindfulness practice.

Chapter 2 Aura Meaning

As you know, all human beings have an aura. The aura is a result of the different chakras rotating inside the body. Each chakra caters to a set number of organs inside the body, which will remain healthy so long as the chakras rotate properly. If there is a blockage in the chakras then the person will develop illnesses and also not have mental clarity.

What are the colors?

There are several colors that the aura can portray at any given point in time. These colors pertain to the individual chakras in the body. Depending on the chakra that is most powerful, the person's aura will take on the particular chakra's color. The different colors are as follows:

The first chakra, also known as the base chakra is colored red. This color will stick to the person's body and denotes the first chakras health. This chakra controls a person's grounding and confidence. If there is a break in the color or there are some black spots in it, then it means that the person has a weak base chakra.

The next chakra is located below the navel and is colored orange. This color sticks to red in the human body. This chakra controls a person's sexuality. If there is a break here or there are spots in the color then it means that the person needs to correct their second chakra in order to avail good health.

The next chakra is the confidence chakra and is located just below the sternum. The color associated with this chakra is yellow. This chakra controls a person's power and confidence. If there is a break in this chakra then it means that the person's third chakra is blocked. This color sticks to the yellow color of the second chakra.

The fourth chakra is the heart chakra. It is located next to the heart. The heart chakra is denoted by the color green. This chakra stands for a person's ability to love and display compassion. A break in this chakra means that the person needs to fix this chakra.

The fifth chakra is located inside the person's throat. This chakra is associated with the color blue. It guides a person's communication skills and self-confidence. A blockage here can result in speech and hearing problems. This color sticks to the person's green color belonging to the fourth chakra.

The sixth chakra is located in between the person's eyebrows where the third eye lies. The color associated with this chakra is indigo. This chakra deals with a person's psychic abilities. A block in this chakra can cause black spots to appear in the indigo ring of the aura.

The last chakra is located inside the person's head and deals with intelligence. The color associated with this chakra is purple. If there is a blockage in this chakra then the person will have a problem concentrating and his or her cognition will be affected.

How is it connected to mindfulness?

The aura and mindfulness are connected at a very deep level. As you know, mindfulness refers to being present in the moment. How the chakras rotate in the body is what will guide a person's mindfulness. The base chakras are the most important chakra and depending on its functioning, the rest of the chakras will rotate inside the body. If the first one has a problem then the last one will also develop a problem. Since the last one deals with intelligence and the mind as a whole, it is extremely important that it remain healthy and rotate optimally. Since all of them are connected like gears, it's vital that that they be fixed, in order to promote mindfulness. In the next , we will read on how you can individually cleanse your aura.

Cleansing aura

The aura in the body plays a very important role. It is meant to supply the body with energy, protection and also holds long-term memories. But our auras can easily get affected by negative influences and absorb other people's negative auras. So it becomes rudimentary to cleanse it from time to time, to get rid of the negativity and remain healthy for long. In this , we will look at how you can cleanse your aura and improve your living.

The aura can be cleansed using certain traditional techniques, which are as follows

Cold shower

The very first remedy to cleanse your aura is to have a cold shower. Most of us prefer to have a hot or tepid shower, as the temperature feels right on our skin. But if you wish to cleanse your aura, then it is best that you make use of a cold shower. You can either stand below the shower or fill up a tub and immerse yourself. For the former you can spend about 10 minutes but for the latter not more than 5 minutes. If you cannot handle too cold then make it slightly warm, not too much though. This is especially recommended if you think you have picked up some sort of negative energy and are feeling down suddenly.

Herbs

Herbs contain a lot of positive energy. You can make use of herbs to cleanse your aura. There are many varieties of herbs available, which you can use and cleanse yourself. Right from frankincense to sage to rosemary, you can add any of the herbs to a bowl and set fire to. Once 3/4ths f it burns, put out the fire and use the bowl to circle around your aura. It will drive all the negativity away and help you cleanse your aura.

Mud therapy

The next therapy is known as mud therapy. Mud therapy is one where you smear pure and natural mud on your body. This will help you get rid of the negative energy in your aura. You can collect some pure mud from your backyard and place it in a bowl. Add in a little spring water to it and make a paste before applying it all over your body. Let it remain for 10 minutes before washing up with cold water.

Crystal healing

Crystal healing is another form of aura cleansing therapy. As you know, crystals contain a low of power and are used to get rid of negative energies. Not only will they purify your aura but also the air around you. Choose a crystal that you think will suit your body. Whether it is sodalite or clear quartz, choose the crystal and place it around your body. You can also place it above your head and make a small pyramid using a piece of cardboard and cover the crystal with it. This will help you trap the energy of the crystal internally.

Sunlight

Sunlight is essential for all living organisms to thrive. But did you know that it is also important for our auras to remain positive. You can stand under the sun for 20 minutes or play some outdoor sports. It is ideal to choose the morning sun as opposed to afternoon sun. Wake up early and get under the sun by 7am. That is when your skin can easily absorb the rays. You can also avail the benefit of absorbing vitamin D.

Salt

Salt is also a good aura cleanser. You can make use of some fresh sea salt to rub over your body. Don't use iodized salt though. Add some to a bowl and stand in the bathroom or shower area. Hold some salt above your head and drop it down. Allow it to fall on your head and then fall off of your body. You can follow it up with a cold shower.

Natural water source

Making use of a natural water source is also a good idea. Whether it's a river or an ocean, get into the water and allow it to cleanse your negative aura. You can also collect the water and add to your tub.

Essential oils

You can make use of essential oils to cleanse your aura as well. There are many types of essential oils like rose, lavender and also vetiver and bay leaf. You can add these to your bath water or can also light a few aromatherapy candles and avail its benefits.

Remember that other people should not be present around when you are cleansing your aura. You must also not use the instruments like the crystals on others before cleansing them thoroughly. You can cleanse them by adding them to a bowl of sea salt or placing them under moonlight.

Daily schedule

You must follow a daily schedule if you wish to remain motivated for long. In this , we will look at a daily schedule that you can employ to increase your mindfulness.

Start with a thought

The very first thing to do is start with a thought. This means that you think of everything that you will do that day. Being present in the moment requires you to think positively. As soon as you wake up, make up your mind on everything that you will do for the day. Remain mindful that you have just woken up and are consciously making a plan. Ensure that you have a smile on your face and are feeling full of life. You can also get up and stretch your entire body as soon as you wake up in the morning.

Mindfully meditate

It is important that you meditate mindfully on a daily basis. As soon as you wake up, start chanting a calming word. You can move around and do some stretching but don't stop meditating. This will help you focus better. You will not feel burdened by everything that you need to do during the day and will feel at peace with yourself.

The word can be anything of your choice and need not always be just "OM". "Love" makes for a good word to mediate upon.

Mindfully finish chores

As you know, you will have to finish a million chores every day. But that does not mean you get carried away and do a shoddy job. Pay keen attention to the chores and ensure that you are fully present in the moment. Don't allow your mind to wander about. From start to finish, you must be present in the moment. You need to focus on the smallest of things that you are doing. Don't think anything is mundane and treat every activity as an important one.

Mindful relaxation

All of us lead hectic lives and need to relax ourselves. It is important that you relax your mind. Don't take everything too seriously and know when to hit the brakes. Try to remain mindful of your situation and see if it is getting a bit too hectic. If it feels cumbersome, then try to distract yourself. You can make use of the mindful counting technique to do so. Mindfulness breathing will also go a long way in helping you relax and feel at peace. In fact, it is best that you schedule your breaks so that you know exactly when to take them.

Mindful conversation

In a day, we meet hundreds of people. Not all of them will play an important role in our lives and so, we need to know who to pay attention to and who not to. Once you know who will be worth paying attention to, you must indulge in mindful conversations. Here, you have to pay attention to what they are saying and reply to them mindfully. Listen to what they have to say to you. Similarly, you must also speak to them mindfully and give them appropriate information.

Mindful exercise

Mindful exercising refers to getting up and exercising a little every now and then. This will ensure that you feel good throughout the day. Tell yourself to get up and perform a certain set of exercises. Have a set number of exercises in your mind and start performing them. Stretch your limbs and take walks. Don't keep sitting in the same place and position, especially at office. You will realize that you are working better and are also able to put in more work. Remain mindful of all your activities through the day.

Have signs

Try to have certain signs around you that will indicate that it is time for you to start performing mindfulness exercises. These can be signs like an alarm or a mail that you send to yourself etc. As soon as these triggers go off, you can start practicing your mindfulness exercises. You can also ask a friend or a co-worker to remind you to perform any of the mindfulness exercises.

Identify triggers

You must identify the different triggers that can cause you stress and anxiety. If you think the trigger has gone off then it is best that you perform the mindfulness exercise. You will feel at peace and the situation will not worsen.

These form the different things that you must do on a daily basis in order to make the habit of mindfulness stick.

Make boring things new

The problem with routine is that it becomes monotonous and boring. Much as we fear change, we also crave it; we like new things and new experiences. Mindfulness is much the same – you can get bored of doing the same exercises again and again. So when you have internalized much of these practices and made mindfulness a way of life, you can start thinking of ways of your own to practice it!

Take for example delivering a lecture to students. If you are going to be traditional, stand in front of a classroom and simply talk, chances are that your students are going to find you boring. You will also get frustrated in that they are not paying attention to you, you are bored, you are actively engaging only a few of your five senses, etc. Instead, use tools like visual aids or storytelling to get the message across – your students will appreciate the newness and the enthusiasm you display! You will be able to mindfully engage them in full – you will listen to what they have to say, see how they respond and feel their enthusiastic energy.

Don't perform your mindfulness exercises by rote memory – find ways to incorporate into your daily life. Don't keep it separate to be performed only at a specific time; as I said, mindfulness is a way of life and has to become part of you to make any palpable sort of a difference.

Remain motivated

When you take up something new, you will have a lot of initial enthusiasm and will manage to perform the task regularly. But as time passes, most of that enthusiasm will die down and you will start feeling lazy. You will wonder if it is best to stop performing the tasks as opposed to performing them half-heartedly. But this is wrong. If you have made up your mind to do something then it is best that you stick with it. Don't think of it as a herculean task and take it slow if you think you are feeling rushed. In this , we will look at how you can remain motivated to perform mindfulness techniques for life.

Take it slow

When it comes to taking up a new activity, don't go about it at super-sonic speed. Don't assume that doing everything fast will help you see faster and better results. In fact, just the opposite might happen and you will give up on it faster than taking it up in the first place. Go about it thoughtfully and instead of unnecessarily rushing into it, set yourself weekly, monthly and yearly goals. As soon as the goal is attained, tick it off and move to the next task. Keep this going until your habit turns into a lifetime choice.

Schedule

Write yourself a set schedule and ensure that you stick with it. As we already saw, you have to write yourself a daily schedule and follow it to a T. Mention clearly the times when you should be getting on with an activity. Provide for a tick box next to it and tick off the activities one by one.

Measure

The very first thing to do to remain motivated is to measure your progress. As you know, it is important to know how much progress you have made since you started with the exercises. Think of how much time you used to spend remaining mindful and how much of a difference has come about since you took it up seriously. Once you understand how much of a difference it has made, you will be motivated to continue with it for a long time.

Reward

It is important to reward yourself from time to time. This reward can be anything that you think will help you remain motivated. It can be gifting yourself something expensive or hitting the spa for a relaxing retreat. As long as it feels good, you can take it up. But don't do it too often, as it will lose its specialty. Affix a certain date in a month and gift yourself your reward.

Partner

Another good way to remain motivated is to find yourself a partner. You and your partner can motivate each other to remain persistent. You can take up the different mindfulness exercises together and exploit them fully. You will not feel like giving up on it easily as that would equate to letting your partner down. This partner can be your friend or sibling or even a colleague. You can also ask your parents to join in if you think they will also benefit from it. Just remember that these people need to join you out of their free will and should not be forced to join in.

Group

It is also a good idea to join a group. This can be a mindfulness group in your area. You can enquire if such a group meets up in your area and join in. You can together indulge in mindfulness exercises. If there is no such group then you can start one yourself. Ask all people interested in mindfulness to join in and start expanding your group. Advertise on social networking sites. Hold regular meditation sessions and also get them to increase their knowledge on the topic by holding talks and presentations.

Research

Conducting constant research on the topic can help you remain motivated. Read on the topic as extensively as possible. Read from the Internet and other books. Ensure that your sources are all reliable and there is no spurious information anywhere. You can ask from an expert for tips and tricks that will help you perform better. If there is something that you can do to enhance your experience like watch a show or documentary on mindfulness then do that. The more you learn the better your chances at remaining put.

These form the different things that you can do to remain motivated and increase your interest in mindfulness.

Chapter 3 Five Steps to Mental Well-being

When people talk of mental well-being, in many instances what comes to mind is depression and stress and other disorders that completely paralyze the normal body functions. Not much though is given to negative emotions that have their source in mind like anger, anxiety, paranoia, fear, frustration, disappointment, hate, and jealousy. All these are emotions that can cripple the mind if not put under control or if they are left to their own devices.

Mindfulness is a practice that brings all these emotions to the forefront and helps you see them for what they are, realize their source, acknowledge the damage they can cause and hence put them into their correct perspective. Your mental well-being allows you to experience life from a happy perspective. However, should you feel that some of these disorders are getting the better part of you, ensure that you get medical assistance from a qualified mental health facility or professional.

Mindfulness focuses on the bigger picture of mental well-being than just treating mental illnesses or avoiding them. It focuses on feeling good about yourself and accepting the world around you as a place of happiness. Physical well-being is not possible to achieve without fully gaining mental well-being, for the simple fact that the mind controls pretty much what happens in your body.

Feelings of satisfaction, enjoyment, harmony, positive involvement with the world, and confidence are, according to part of the whole of mental well-being. It is a state that boosts your self-esteem and confidence and makes you feel that you can actually do the things you want to because the only hindrance to achieving your goals, after all, is YOU. The only way to get over that hindrance is to muster your emotions and mental processes.

Mental well-being does not by any means insinuate that you will not have moments when you will experience moments of difficulty and situations that appear as if they want to drain you completely. What happens is that when you are faced with such emotions, you will always find the resilience and courage to cope with them.

Society's View of Mental Well-being

Studies show that a majority of people tend to associate wealth with mental well-being, but the situation on the ground is purely contrary to this belief. In Britain for example, over the last fifty years, it is clear that life has improved financially for many people, but when those same people were asked to rate their state of mental well-being, it becomes evidently clear that mental well-being has deteriorated.

This is a clear indication that the things people hold in high regard as the source of a healthy mental well-being do not give lasting solutions. In other words, mental well-being is not just about you own materially, but is more abstract, more about being in touch with innermost being and personality. This is why it is important to practice mindfulness, as this meditation technique will help you reach your innermost being with ease.

Evidence of Mental Well-being

People all around the world have an assortment of practices to help them reach a point of achieving mental well-being. Some are steeped in religion while others take a new age approach to meditation and even exercise. Mindfulness is one of the techniques that has proven to be excellent for developing mental well-being.

To find out how other techniques are working for people, it is important to observe them. Observation shows that people who have come to a point of self-realization live happier lives and are able to handle any kind of situation that comes their way without getting an overhaul of emotions, be they positive or negative.

It has also been found that mental well-being can be measured by exposing groups of people to various life circumstances. The key again is to observe how they would respond to them or handle a situation of pressure or conflict. This is done by asking a series of questions to find out how the respondents feel about themselves and whether they are living in a conscious state of mindfulness or mindlessness.

Here are some specific steps that you can take towards achieving a status of mental well-being through the practice of mindfulness.

Become Curious and Connect

While there is the type of curiosity that killed the cat, there is a healthy curiosity that leads you to develop an interest in learning new things in matters of well-being. Remember that no one can hand curiosity to you on a silver platter, so you have to take action to gain it from within.

You need to want to know how you can make the most of mindfulness. Understanding the basis of how mindfulness should spark some curiosity within you, making it possible for you to find success through this meditation.

Once curiosity builds up within you, it is time to join hands with other people who practice the art of mindfulness and learn from them. You will realize that it becomes easier to practice when you have internal and external support, but even without a group with common interests, be sure not to stop at anything less until you achieve your goals.

Look for people who practice mindfulness techniques at group meetings or join some forums online. The more you open your mind, the easier it is for your thoughts to manifest and give you even more ideas of where you can find like-minded people.

Remaining active is the name of the game.

Just like any other goal, you have in life and which you have to put effort into every single day, the same goes for the art of mindfulness. For starters, it may be hard to do the same thing day in day out because as you may well know, routine can be boring. This can be curbed by incorporating exercises in your meditation. Find an activity that you enjoy doing and do it before or after your meditation session.

Being active physically goes a long way in improving your mental health as well. Ensure that you incorporate mindful walking, mindful eating, and mindfulness in breathing, mindful compassion, mindfulness in thoughts, mindfulness of your body and external world, mindfulness of relationships, mindfulness of leadership and mindfulness of emotions in every instance of your life.

Sounds overwhelming when you look at it like this, but all that it really requires is for you to appreciate what it means to be present - and embrace it.

Learn something new about mindfulness on a daily basis.

If you have successfully managed to cultivate your curiosity on the issue of mindfulness, you will find within you there is a never-ending desire to learn more and more about becoming a fully established individual who is rooted in mindfulness. You can learn something new from your environment, or you can choose to expand your scope of learning by getting in touch with masters of the art of mindfulness.

Signing up for courses that teach you the deeper doctrines of mindfulness, and its relationship to other doctrines that are meditation-based will do you a lot of good. In such classes, you will meet people with different experiences in the course of practicing mindfulness and their experiences will teach you a thing or two about the art, and the importance of looking out for your mental well-being.

Giving

You may not have given thought to this, but did you know that just being good to others and giving your kindness, patience and even material things counts a lot in relaxing your mind? This will give you an immediate sense of joy, affecting both your outer behavior and your inner thoughts.

Do you know that what you give to others does not have to cost you a fortune for your to feel satisfied and for your mind to be refreshed? Do you also know that you do not have to dwell on that moment of accomplishment but you can create many more such moments by practicing the art of giving? What you give could be as simple as a smile to a child who needs it, or just a kind word to a grumpy person at work or across the street. Larger acts of giving can be volunteering your time and services for the benefit of the larger society.

When you practice giving, allow yourself to be present and to rest in all the positive thoughts that will go through your mind.

Choosing Mindfulness

If you ask people who have never heard about the art of mindfulness what being mindful is all about, some would tell you that it is giving thoughts to other people, to your actions, and being cautious about how you live your life. While this might have some truth to it, being mindful is a lot deeper than this because it makes you become more aware of your circumstances.

It has a lot more to do with yourself, than with other people or circumstances around you. Once you attain a state of mindfulness, you tend to throw caution to the wind to some extent. Why? Because you are aware of your inner being, and you have gained the ability to get over negative emotions that drive people to hurt others.

You do not need to be considerate because within you, only the good forces of love, kindness and compassion rule in you. Being considerate therefore comes naturally. In a deeper sense, it is like you are automated to responding positively to every present moment and hence you will never have regrets and apologies to deal with once you have fully acquired a state of mindfulness.

Chapter 4 How Can Mindfulness Help You Find Inner Peace?

Some of us can spend all our lives looking for inner peace. While there are those who can find it, sadly there are also those who cannot. Mindfulness is a great way to achieve that inner happiness and calmness so many wish they could have. In order to understand how to find your inner peace through mindfulness practice, it is important to understand one thing. What exactly is inner peace?

Basically, inner peace is the absence of internal (and even external) suffering. Sometimes, the terms true happiness and inner peace can be used interchangeably. Although they are similar, there is a slight difference between the two. True happiness means that there is a connection or an element of joy or excitement. Happiness is an emotion arising from inner peace. That means that inner peace itself is finding complete and utter contentment with one's life.

In order to achieve inner peace, one must understand what suffering is. Practitioners of mindfulness know that there are four Noble Truths associated with suffering. We will briefly define them now.

The first of the four noble truths is the actual existence of suffering. Everyone is well aware of the fact that suffering exists. Some people feel it on a deeper level than others, but it is there in most of us nonetheless. For the majority of us, it tends to be slight mental, emotional or even physical anguish. If one has a conscious mind and emotions, they are capable of suffering. One cannot find true inner peace until they are able to overcome suffering and find a way to become more resilient to it.

The second noble truth is the origins of suffering. With this, we see varying ideas on where suffering actually originated from. It could be the result of becoming attached or clinging to another. It could be ignorance. It could be a combination of both. What it boils down to is that it came from somewhere. It is natural for humans to become attached to people or things that give us emotional gratification or pleasure. People become attached to others, places, memories and even beliefs. The things we become attached to fulfil some deep rooted need that we've come to believe is necessary for us to be happy. When something we've become attached to is lost, we suffer.

The third noble truth is ending suffering. Here, we see that it is possible to live a life free of suffering. We can do this by developing a greater inner awareness and mindfulness. While this can be easier said than done, with practice and determination, it is entirely possible to achieve. True mindfulness helps us be aware of our actions and the consequences associated with them. In learning this, we can start to behave in ways that ultimately have less suffering for us and the people we love.

The final and fourth truth is the path that leads to ending suffering. Here, there are eight principles one must live by in order to end their suffering. They are:

Having the right view of life. This does not mean your view is more valuable or correct than another. Having the right view is basically having a positive outlook on life and the world around you. Positivity is important in mindfulness. Negative emotions and ideas tend to block one from being able to find that inner peace they need. When using mindful meditation, you will recognize these thoughts and learn to stop them in their tracks before they get out of control. Positivity is always the answer.

The right way of thinking. This goes along with positivity and finding the good in other people and the world around you. It has less to do with political or religious views and more to do with focus, finding the bright side and that ever important positivity.

The right speech. What you say and how your words are spoken have a great impact on inner peace. In this instance, knowing not to say anything hurtful or cruel is key. In the heat of the moment, that can be hard. What's important is to try to practice this on a daily basis. Find something positive to say to your friend, family or even a complete stranger. It's a pretty great feeling to see them smile and know you had something to do with brightening someone else's day.

The right action. We all know the difference between right and wrong. Acting with purpose and positivity is something we should all practice regularly. The phrase do the right thing is accurate when speaking of the right action.

The right livelihood. This is one of the most important of the eight principles one should live by. The right livelihood involves finding a path in life that does not compromise one's ethics. What you choose to do for work in particular should not bring harm to others. This is tough because many large businesses are globalized these days. Not many people can up and leave a well-paying job, either. Working ethically within an organization is a great way to practice integrity, decency and honesty without having to find another job.

The right effort. This can go hand in hand with one's job, or everyday life. As long as an honest effort is made, that's what counts. This will be the same with your practice. In the beginning, it will be difficult. As long as an effort is being made, you are on the right path.

The right concentration. This tends to come with practice. Concentrating on meditation in a thoughtful manner is one way to get to the right concentration. As with most things in life, it will take practice. When we concentrate, thoughts that shouldn't be there might make an appearance. Realize that this is part of the process and that it is okay and then move on.

The right mindfulness. The final step in this process is achieving the right mindfulness that will help one let go of their suffering and get on the path to finding their inner peace.

Now that we have talked about suffering and how to overcome it, let's talk about the ways that achieving mindfulness can help one find inner peace.

A lot of us carry suffering and pain from previously unresolved issues in our pasts. It can be anything from a bad relationship to traumatic experiences or even the loss of a loved one. The list is extensive, but it comes down to those experiences being an obstacle to achieving happiness. Until we are able to transform them, we will not be able to find the true inner peace we seek. Mindfulness meditation can help heal the wounds from the past. It aids in understanding painful situations and helps one to see things from a different, broader perspective. It helps to realize that we are not the only people who have suffered, which in turn, grows your compassion toward others. With that, inner strength will also increase, with practice, which diminishes pain and suffering, replacing it with love, peace and acceptance.

Mindfulness can also help improve relationships. It does not matter how much life experience we have, when it comes to relationships, we can always find ways to improve. Communication is key to healthy, long-lasting relationships and that will bring greater harmony and peace to those relationships. Mindfulness meditation has several tools to use that will aid in relationships. Mindful speech and deep listening are two great ways to help reduce misunderstandings that can lead to conflict. The ability to forgive and be nonjudgmental are two more ways we can improve relationships. The inner strength gained from meditating mindfully will make all of these things easier. In turn, it will enable one to develop a deeper compassion for people and bring more intimacy and love into the relationship.

Meditation is wonderful for aging and overall better health. Unfortunately, we all age and our health declines. It can be anything from the normal wear and tear of aging to serious illnesses. Whatever the case may be, it is a reminder of mortality and how fragile life can be. Mindfully meditating can help deal with aging and health issues. Accepting the fact that you are aging is a huge step. Keep emotions calm and develop inner strength. We know that there is research to show that mindfulness meditation can help reduce stress, which is one of the major contributors to poor health. Practice also improves the immune system, which is important for quicker healing and resistance to many sicknesses and diseases. Mindfulness helps one to realize that they are more than just their body and mind, that they are connected to the rest of humanity and nature on a deeper level. This helps to abate loneliness and insecurity, enabling one to live their life to the fullest.

All of these things working together will not only improve overall health, it helps to find that inner peace so many seek. It is a rare thing to discover and with proper practice with mindfulness meditation, it is entirely possible.

Chapter 5 Awakening and Meta-Awareness

Years of conditioning has taught us that we must eliminate our flaws, ignore uncomfortable feelings and strong arm our way into places we feel are more pleasant or good to flatter our self-image. We have an instinctual fight or flight response that helps us to avoid threats, whether they are real or imagined, to our wellbeing and safety. This response is neurological in nature and is what has ensured our survival for the past million years or so. Although it is responsible for our longevity over a millennia, if it is left unchecked, it can undermine soulful aspects of what makes us unique. What we need to do is accept ourselves the way we are as opposed to trying to fix or change whatever we do not like.

Mindfulness can help us know, accept and value ourselves by taking a moment to look at ourselves from the inside and see exactly what we are feeling and experiencing from one moment to the next. Instead of deciding that there is anything wrong with us because of uneasy or troublesome feelings or thoughts, we just need to acknowledge the things we do notice. Observe and accept. Psychologist Tara Brach refers to this as radical acceptance and it is an incredibly freeing feeling. We are able to take that moment and experience it as it is without judgement or resentment.

Accepting ourselves for who and what we are includes embracing whatever experience we have. It helps us to expand our tolerance for the experience and observe how things are coming and going. Whatever we are experience, and this may include all unpleasant feelings, pass more easily if we are able to relate to them in a friendly and accepting way. It is then we can notice settling of our experiences.

In order to be mindful, we need to be completely present. Those of us who practice mindful meditation know that it does lead to a greater calmness or insight. Research done on this type of meditation has been shown to be helpful in reducing stress, pain, anxiety, depression and several other ailments. Actually practicing mindfulness is not about the science or the research, though. It is about connecting with ourselves on a deep level. It is about understanding our psyche. It is about acceptance. And, perhaps most importantly, it is about being non-judgmental.

It is particularly important to reiterate how non-judgment is crucial. It is actually one of the major components in raising your level of awareness as well as being able to enjoy the benefits. This is achieved by the practice of watching your own thoughts, reactions, feelings and all other experiences as they enter into your consciousness.

In order to cultivate mindfulness, there needs to be a temporary suspension of inner judgment. It needs to happen. You need to let it happen and simply watch. To do this, you must maintain focus on the moment as it happens. Our day to day awareness is overcome by our plans for the future and our memories of the past. It is difficult to stop this kind of thinking, which can make it difficult to sleep or even relax. At our basic level, awareness is grounded in what we are experiencing in that moment.

That can lead to quite the precarious situation. Because our awareness is often occupied with memories of the past and thoughts of our futures, the mind is on a constant loop, focusing solely on those two things. Obviously, the future and our memories are extremely important. The past is part of who we are today and the future is where our dreams and aspirations live. We would not be much of a person if we didn't have and recognize those. The experiences in the present moment is where we are able to strengthen our awareness and is where mindfulness can truly begin.

The essence in practicing mindful meditation is building what is referred to as meta-awareness. When we are in a state of normal awareness, it is a constant stream of feelings and thoughts that are associated with our sense of self. This may be on a conscious level, or we might not be aware of it. With meta-awareness, you are able to view those feelings and thoughts with detachment. You can observe them for what they are...thoughts and feelings unassociated with yourself. With enough practice, meta-awareness gives us the chance to look at ourselves objectively.

To break this down further, meta-awareness is what fosters one's presence. A person's presence is felt rather than seen. To feel it in another person is just knowing that they have a deeper peace and inner calm within them. That is their presence and some people are able to make it more known than others. Those are the people who practice mindful meditation and either have, or are close to mastering it.

Being able to experience this firsthand is an incredibly powerful experience. You are able to understand yourself on that deep level that most other people cannot. You will feel more at ease with yourself and find that life has grace, purpose even. With mindfulness meditation and some greatly disciplined effort, that presence we've spoken of can be created internally and then felt both by yourself and others.

One of the main questions about mindfulness meditation is whether or not it needs to be practiced on a daily basis. Does it mean you can never just let go and have some mindless fun? Not at all. Theoretically speaking, most people probably spend less than one-percent of their day being mindful. The other ninety-nine percent of the time is spent on the normal state of awareness and thoughts of past and present. If you were able to find forty-five minutes to an hour to devote to this each day, just think of what it could do for your mental state, your overall health and your relationships. In the grand scheme of things, that isn't a whole lot of time to devote. You aren't spending hours upon hours each day trying to attain that mindful, meditative state.

That sense of awakening and meta-awareness one can achieve with mindful meditation is, as we've mentioned, great for people in all aspects of their lives. It isn't something that takes up a tremendous amount of time. Besides, who can't use an hour to themselves each day? Finding a quiet spot to just relax and observe your inner self without criticism can be a fantastic way to start or end your day.

Chapter 6 Benefits of Meditation

If you were to research the benefits of meditation, you would literally see thousands of results. The benefits seem never ending, which is a good sign, right? That means that the time it takes to meditate mindfully each day is nothing compared to all the great things it will do for your mind and body. In this , we are going to cover the top reasons meditation is beneficial. If you aren't already convinced, you will be by the time you are done with this .

Not only have Buddhists been using this for centuries, there is scores of scientific research to back up the benefits of mindful meditation. Meditation in general, too. We are going to look at several fantastic reasons meditation is such a great practice to incorporate in your daily life.

It is proven to lower stress. Although practitioners have known this for years...centuries even, recent scientific research recently published shows how mindfulness reduces stress. It not only helps the person to feel less stressed, it also reduces the levels of cortisol, the hormone that causes stress in the human body.

It helps us get to know our true selves. The art of mindfulness allows us to see past the rose-colored glasses we use on a daily basis. Without those in place, we are able to analyze ourselves objectively. A study released by the Psychological Science journal showed that mindfulness can help people conquer blind spots that either diminish or amplify our flaws exponentially.

Meditation can help improve grades in school. Another study done in California showed that college students who used mindfulness actually did better in the verbal reasoning portion of their GRE. They also improved their working memory, which in turn improved their test scores and overall grades.

It changes the brain protectively. As we in one, science has proven that mindful meditation affects certain parts of the brain. In particular, the flight or fight part of the brain, which is also where stress is centered. This part of the brain decreases while the grey matter portion of the brain (where logic and reasoning is stored) grows larger.

Meditation can reduce the chances of mental illness. While some are hereditary, research at the University of Oregon has shown that mindful meditation can actually combat mental illness. Meditation increased connections in the brain known as axonal density. It also increased the myelin or protective tissue that surround axons in the brain. Basically, it helped decrease these markers for mental diseases.

It can help with brain volume. Meditation helps people to feel that Zen like state. With enough practice, the brain can better control pain and emotions and how they are processed.

Meditational elements and health benefits. These benefits are broken down into four parts. Body awareness, regulation of attention, regulation of emotion and self-awareness. Being aware of these in general is great for one's overall health both physically and mentally.

It can make you a better person. Meditation does wonderful things for us and our bodies. But, it can also be beneficial to the people we interact with on a daily basis. Mindful meditation makes us more compassionate toward others. It has also been linked to the 'do-gooder' behavior.

Meditation can help with cancer treatment. Surprisingly enough, art therapy combined with mindful meditation has shown a decrease in the stress women with breast cancer experience. Imaging has also shown brain changes related to emotions and reward as well as stress.

It can help the elderly. The aging population suffers a great deal of depression. Their friends and mate may have passed on leaving them to feel alone. Most elderly do not reach out to others for help or to discuss these problems because that is not what their generation was taught to do. They were always taught to grin and bear it, which isn't a great thing for one's psyche. Loneliness has been known to cause a great deal of health conditions in the elderly, including depression. Mindfulness meditation helped to ease these feelings of loneliness and sadness, which was able to boost their overall health.

Meditation can help alleviate cold and flu symptoms. During the colder seasons, good hygiene is crucial to keeping the cold and flu virus at bay. However, that isn't always enough. Studies have shown that meditation coupled with exercise can actually decrease the effects of colds. That means the body aches and fevers might be lessened, or the time you suffer could be shorter. Regardless, those studies showed that people who practiced meditation regularly missed less days at work. Their symptoms were also less severe.

It can help with weight loss goals. When coupled with diet and exercise, mindful meditation can actually help give you that extra boost you need to get to your goal weight. Seven out of ten psychologists in a study said that mindfulness meditation provided a great added strategy when it came to weight loss.

Meditation can lower the risk of depression in pregnant women and teens. With pregnant women, studies have shown that they may benefit from mindfulness meditation in the way of yoga. There are very few drugs that pregnant women can take to help with the symptoms of depression. What's great about yoga and mindful meditation is that they are natural ways to decrease the feelings of despair and sadness that sometimes comes with being pregnant. Recent studies have shown that as many as one in five pregnant women are diagnosed with depression. When it comes to teenagers, mindfulness can reduce anxiety, stress and depression.

It can help you sleep better. We would be remiss to not mention one of the greatest benefits of mindful meditation. Not only does it help to control emotions, moods and stress, it can help get a great night sleep. With less stress and better control over your emotions, your mind is easier to shut down at night because it can let go of the events of the day or week.

As at the beginning of this , these are just a few of the great benefits of using mindful meditation. There are quite literally hundreds, if not thousands more benefits. Now that we've made a believer out of you, let's get into the basics of mindfulness practice. In the final , we will detail mindful meditation so that by the end of this book, you will be ready to embark on your own meditational adventure.

Chapter 7 How Mindfulness can save Relationships

When you have the wrong state of mind, it affects your life in many ways and more so in your relationships. Mindfulness, on the other hand, encourages you to pay attention to your feelings in relation to other people.

This is best explained with an example. Imagine that you are angry at your spouse because they did not meet their part of responsibility as far as parenting your children is concerned. Perhaps your spouse was supposed to pay for some service at a school for your child but did not do it. In addition, there could have been a breakdown in communication so that you did not find out about this until your child was unable to take part in the activity.

Your mind will go into overdrive, and you will likely feel anger, frustration and disappointment. Your thoughts may be that you are unable to trust your partner with parenting and simple things. You will be upset that your child had to miss out on an activity. You may feel as though you have all this weight on your shoulders.

If you do not get the chance to discuss this incident with your spouse and deal with it once and for all, chances are that communication between the two of you will negatively be affected. So how does mindfulness come in to help you save a situation that is fast spiraling out of control?

As stated earlier in the introductory , mindfulness has a history that is borrowed from the religion of Buddhism, and more specifically, from a concept of Buddhism known as dharma. Dharma has given rise to other forms of meditation like Chan in Chinese or Zen in Japanese.

Mindfulness is today a milder form of Zen or Chan, as it more about lifestyle than it is about religion or doctrinal teachings. In fact, more books have been written on the concept of Dharma since the 5th Century than on

Mindfulness, which is a relatively new concept compared to the mainstream Buddhism.

However, there are concepts that can be borrowed from Buddhism meditation and which work as effectively in mindfulness meditation. Here are a few things that you can borrow from Buddhism for effective mindfulness in relation to establishing workable relationships.

Exploration of Relationships

Mindfulness is about living in the present, and this is also applicable to relationships. Purposely bring your mind to a state of making an inventory of your relationships. Explore them one by one, because the way you relate with your spouse is different from the way you relate to your children or your parents.

Cultivate a genuine interest to deepen the level of relatedness. During this journey you may realize that you have been taking you children for granted at times; putting their need for spending time with you as their parent somewhere in the middle or bottom of your priority list. All this will be in your thoughts, and when you take the time to become present, even those that have been pushed to the back of your mind will find their way forward and present themselves to you.

As you do this, avoid the temptation of falling into cultural, social or intellectual explanations of what relationships are supposed to look like and how they are supposed to work. Remember that mindfulness is about an individual experience and so are relationships. Allow your thoughts to heighten your awareness, and this will clarify how you can build your relationships.

Becoming genuinely interested in the nature of your relationships

When you practice mindfulness meditation, you will honestly establish why you are in your relationship. This will help you determine how much of your relationship is rooted in love. Some of the questions that could arise for you include; is your relationship for mutual advantage or are you in it because your spouse genuinely affects your world in a positive way? If you were to choose your spouse now, would they be the same all over again?

Here is where you need to be very honest with yourself. Bring your relationship into the present realm and allow your mind to ascertain what is working, and where you need to improve.

Once you have successfully gone through the above techniques, the next step is in working on your findings through the following techniques in order to arrive at the ideal situation of your relationships. This is the state in which you are able to experience every little detail of your relationships at the present moment.

Practising Mindfulness to Decrease Stress in relationships

Relationships can cause you considerable stress but sometimes the major reason for the stress is that we do not pay attention to living in the present. How many times have you heard of people having a disagreement where one party brings out an aspect from the past where they had another argument for different reasons?

This clearly tells you that the party bringing up issues from the past is still living in the past and not giving attention to what is happening in the present. If whenever you have a disagreement with people in your life, you focus on the present, chances are that you are on the way to creating very happy and healthy relationships.

Mindfulness meditation encourages you to remain in the present and helps you learn to live with your past.

Mindfulness is a technique through which you understand the needs of the people in your relationships

After looking closely at the relationships that have the most meaning to you, it is time to consider how much effort you put into ensuring that those relationships are well nurtured. Nurturing of relationships requires that you meet the needs of those people you are in the relationship and more specifically, the needs of the people most close to you.

You need to practice being present in your relationships as this equates to mindfulness. This means that when you are spending time with your family, do not allow yourself to be engrossed or distracted with other activities. This is especially important when you are in the middle of a discussion.

How does it feel when you are talking to someone and they are busy on their computer on or their phone? Feels like you are being ignored, right? That person has not developed the art of living in the moment and you will notice that they miss out on a lot of fantastic moments.

Appreciating the good moments in relationships

Someone once said that gratitude determines your attitude. In other words, how grateful you are for the things in your life, relationships included, determines how far you go with those things or how much you even enjoy them.

The more grateful you are for the people in your life, the more you will enjoy spending time with them, but this will only be possible if you pay real attention to what you are doing while you are together.

When you do something with the people who mean a lot to you and do it in full awareness of the moment, nothing beats this experience and you will strive to make this a habit. This will go a long way in making your relationships more worthwhile, and the more sense you get out of them, the more thankful you will be for those relationships and the more you will give them your very best.

You will ensure that your mind does not drift into thinking about other things that you should be doing or other places you should be at because you are in the present moment, fully aware of it and enjoying every bit of it. The more you practice the technique of being thankful, not just in relationships but in other aspects of life, the more aware you will become of your life.

Chapter 8 Why Practice Mindfulness?

The thing with mindfulness is that some of the most popular opinions regarding it are completely wrong. People put too much flair to it or have expectations that are absurd or unrealistic. Mindfulness is not supposed to fix you magically... for example, if you have depression, mindfulness will certainly help you become more peaceful. But you also need to take the necessary steps to deal with depression.

Here are five things that far too many people get wrong about mindfulness:

Mindfulness is not about "fixing you."

Mindfulness has never been about stopping one's thoughts

Mindfulness belongs to no religion.

Mindfulness is not meant to help you escape from reality

Mindfulness is no panacea

With all this in mind, why practice mindfulness? There are numerous reasons why you should practice mindfulness on the regular, as mentioned in the . Mindfulness has been proven to improve lives as well as boost, among other aspects of health, and one's mental health.

Here are the top reasons why you should subscribe to the practice of mindfulness:

1: Mindfulness alleviates stress or at the very least some of it

We presently live in a "generation of stress." There is a lot of pressure on people today, and this often leads to a lot of accumulated stress. Stress will usually lead to health problems. At the very least, your mental health will suffer. Mindfulness is a great stress-prevention tool. People who practice mindfulness admit to feeling less stressed as they handle the issues that life serves them.

2: Mindfulness is more than just reducing stress levels

Certainly, stress reduction comes with mindfulness. However, the ultimate goal is not to reduce stress. The ultimate goal of mindfulness is to trigger the motion of our inner mental, emotional, and physical states. The goal is to make you more alive and more functional "in the present."

3: Mindfulness trains your body to thrive

You need to look no further than professional athletes for proof of this. Many pro athletes use mindfulness meditation to encourage peak performance. Collegiate basketball players are being coached to accept negative thoughts meditatively and transmute them into positive ones. Cycling champions have been coached to follow their breath for decades now. Big wave surfers are encouraged to brood on and transform their fears.

Sports psychologists have described these mindful techniques as being vital in the "coaching of the whole person." Once your mind is set right by mindfulness, it follows that your body will also be primed to perform at its best.

4: Mindfulness boosts creativity

Whether your art of choice is coloring, drawing writing, music, Etc., all of them have meditative practices that accompany them. The more 'present' you are, the more free your mind is and this can allow for more creative juices to flow.

5: Mindfulness strengthens your neural connections

By training your brain in mindfulness, you can build new neural pathways as well as networks in your brain, which helps you boost concentration, awareness, flexibility, and many other cognitive abilities.

6: Mindfulness reduces over-thinking and rumination

Often, what underlies anxiety is the unsavory duo of rumination and over-thinking. Once you worry about something, the brain is designed to commit to clinging onto the thing. It is very easy to be caught in a loop that has you replay every bad outcome that is possible, and this is not beneficial at all. Mindfulness helps you cease the endless worry and instead focus on the present.

7: Mindfulness boosts memory, focus, and performance

Being able to pay attention and focus on tasks at hand has to be one of the most vital cognitive abilities a human being can have. Seeing as mindfulness helps prevent mind-wandering and cluttering, it also helps you stay in the moment. You can give your undivided attention to the issues at hand. You are better able to focus on and solve problems competently.

8: Mindfulness helps greatly with emotional reactivity

Mindfulness helps you stay in the present. It makes you a "now" person. One perk that stems from this is that you are less emotionally reactive. You feel less compelled to recoil emotionally at every other thing that prods at you. You are better able to roll with the punches and only respond to those things that warrant it.

9: Mindfulness upholds cognitive flexibility

A study suggests that the practice of mindfulness not only helps you become less emotionally reactive; it also adds to your cognitive flexibility. If you observe most people that practice mindfulness (especially those who are great proponents of meditation as a tool to hone their mindfulness), you may notice that they are also great at self-observation that promptly disengages those pathways that were forged in the brain from prior incidences of learning; thus allowing incoming information to be understood in new, innovative ways.

10: Improves your general emotional health

By focusing on the present and affirming to yourself that indeed, you are valuable and effective in the present moment, you improve your self-image. You can adopt a more positive outlook on life. Two studies conducted on mindfulness meditation recorded decreased depression in more than 4,600 adults.

A study followed some 18 volunteer adults as they practiced mindfulness meditation for three years. This study unearthed that depression decreased and that these cases of reduced depression were long term in nature.

Further, cytokines, which are inflammatory chemicals that are released in response to stress may affect your mood and eventually lead to depression. A review of multiple studies suggested that mindfulness meditation could reduce depression by decreasing these chemicals.

11: Reduction in Age-related memory loss

Improvements in focus and attention, as well as clarity of thought, may play a major role in keeping your mind young. And when your mind is young, your body tends to stay young as well.

Kirtan Kriya is a mindfulness meditation technique which combines a chant or mantra with repetitive finger motions in a bid to focus your thoughts. In numerous cases of age-based memory loss, this technique helped improve participants' ability to do memory retention tasks.

What is more, a review of 12 studies discovered that multiple styles of mindfulness meditation elevated attention, speed of thought, and comprehension in older volunteer adults.

12: Mindfulness enables you to fight addictions better

The mental discipline and resolve that you develop through mindfulness meditation may help you deal with dependencies better. By practicing mindfulness, you are better equipped to face them head-on and break them. Your superior self-control and awareness will help you cut out addictions easier.

Research has shown that mindfulness meditation may help you learn to redirect your attention as well as boost your willpower. You will be in a better position to control your emotions as well as your impulses. Through time, you will be able to increase your understanding of the causes behind your most addictive behaviors.

One study which taught 19 recovering alcoholics meditation techniques showed that the participants who took in training and tried to apply it responded far better to their cravings compared to those that did not.

13: Mindfulness can help you handle pain better

Your perception of pain is connected to your mental state. In stressful conditions, it may be elevated.

For instance, a study used functional MRI techs in a bid to observe the activity of the brain as the participants experienced pain. Some of the participants had undergone as many as four days of mindfulness meditation training. The others had no meditation training.

The patients that had meditation training showed increased activity in the brain centers responsible for pain-control. They also reported less pain sensitivity.

With those amazing benefits you stand to benefit by practicing mindfulness, let us now learn how actually to practice mindfulness so that you know what to do to enjoy the amazing benefits this practice has to offer.

Chapter 9 Simple Mindful Meditation Techniques

One possible definition of meditation is the systematic training of the mind to focus inward thereby bringing it under our conscious control. For many beginners, meditation can be frustrating and difficult causing undue stress as opposed to relaxation.

The mind is active, constantly seeking to understand, examine, and discuss. This becomes all the more apparent when we try to sit still for some time. There is a common misconception that we do meditation in order to silence the mind, however this is actually a byproduct of meditation, not the goal.

To use force on the mind to silence the mind using the mind is a contradiction and generally leads to frustration and discontent. A friendlier way of approaching meditation is to think of our time on the cushion as a practice of observing the mind. With less ambition and more determination we are cultivating curiosity and awareness rather than force.

If one wishes to learn to ski, we do not start by going straight to the most difficult obstacle course and trail, instead we focus on our technique. We practice basic maneuvers on the "bunny slopes" and then gradually make our way to the more difficult trails. Similar in meditation, one must develop the groundwork and maneuvers in order to progress and learn.

Here are a few simple meditation techniques that provide training for the mind, allowing us to relax and enjoy meditation. Try one, or several of these techniques and once you find one that works, practice it consistently and frequently - results will come.

Single Object Meditation: Start with something simple and not overly graphic, like a candle or a pen. Begin to gently gaze at this object and think about the object, the structure, the shape, color, size, anything that is related to the object. As you do this, feel yourself becoming physically and emotionally entangled with the object.

After a comfortable time gazing, close your eyes and see the object in your mind's eye. Hold it there for as long as you can until it begins to get fuzzy or starts to fade. Once you have determined that it has faded, or is significantly altered so that you have to imagine or recall from memory the object, open your eyes and repeat the process again.

I find that very visual people are able to do this easily and find this exercise to be fun and non-visual people have a very difficult time holding the object for even five seconds.

If you are one of those people who have a very difficult time with this, keep practicing on a regular basis and you will improve dramatically. This is a preliminary exercise and can be beneficial to practice for a few weeks before trying the other three techniques.

Develop the Watcher: Take a small part of your attention and assign this part the task of watching everything that flutters through the mind - without judgment or criticism. Imagine this part as a video camera that records everything, to be stored and analyzed almost immediately after it occurs.

As you begin to develop this ability, you can notice thoughts, stories, narratives, emotions, reactions, and many other processes going on in your mind. This form of meditation, sometimes referred to as mindfulness can be practiced anywhere and anytime.

It is essential that we do not criticize or condemn what we see, imply observe and grow in awareness and depth. With clear awareness, comes insight, understanding, and the power to change.

Mantras: A powerful and easy technique to conquer internal dialogue is to repeat a words or phrases over and over again. By concentrating the mind on these specific words, all other thoughts are cast aside.

There are many sacred mantras that exist in the world but the most important factor in choosing a mantra is that we cultivate an attitude of deep reverence for the words - as if they are sacred. In some traditions, mantras are whispered into students' ears and the students is to keep this mantra secret and never speak it out loud.

With time and practice, the mind will begin to quiet down and only the breath and the mantra will be heard. Once this state is achieved, there is no more need to for the mantra because all intruding thoughts have been cast out.

Over time, just a few conscious breaths and the thought of the mantra should be enough to clear the mind. Clearing the mind is of course not the end goal of meditation, rather, it is the state that enables you to begin meditation; this is where deep self-exploration begins.

Breath Awareness: Once a comfortable and steady upright posture is established, bring the attention to the belly. Notice how it rises and falls. In the beginning, one or both palms can be placed on the abdomen to bring awareness to the sensations there.

Focus the mind on the breath as it moves in and out, and as soon as the mind becomes distracted, without judgment or distress bring it back to the belly and the breath.

This is probably the simplest and one of the most commonly used meditation techniques in the world. Breath awareness and mantra repetition can be combined to further train and focus the mind. One example would be to say "In" on the in-breath and "Out" on the out-breath.

MEDITATION TECHNIQUES

Mind is a wonderful instrument available to us, which allows us to experience emotions, sensations and to perceive, through the five senses, everything that surrounds us. But to be happy and live in a peaceful condition we need to control the mind to prevent it from conditioning us too much and from repressing our freedom. Human mind never stops, it is frenetic and imperative, so to control it we must begin to know it, observing it and understanding it. To do so we must first of all learn to control our senses, hearing, smell, touch, taste and sight. They are not reliable, they can deceive us and the more we practice, the more we become aware of this and of all that is around us.

By controlling our senses we will learn also to control our thoughts, and to do all this we need meditation.

In the   we have already addressed the subject of meditation, mentioning some techniques and linking it to the breathing we talked about in the . In this new , however, we will try to better understand what meditation is and how it can be practiced, going into more detail, to improve our lives and lead us to achieve inner peace.

Meditation therefore, is a practice that allows us to elevate our vital state, increase our positive energies and, most of all, to learn to master our mind. Meditation is the fulcrum of most Eastern religions, or of all religions, but in this context we use meditation as a practice to improve the relationship with ourselves and with the environment that surrounds us; the religious aspect is a purely personal choice. Meditation in Eastern philosophy. but also in mindfulness philosophy, is a tool to know ourselves in depth, to achieve self-awareness until we can reach the inner peace, which occurs when our mind is calm and silent. This practice can also be simply used as a relaxation technique, especially at the beginning of the meditative journey.

There are a lot of meditative techniques, and soon we will list some of them so that we can put them into practice right away.

Knowing ourselves, creating a bridge between the external self and our deepest being, is not a trivial matter and, above all, a lot of practice and perseverance are necessary, but once we have mastered ourselves we will be able to obtain a temple in our mind, full of peace and balance, in which to know how to master anxiety, stress, nervousness etc.

As mentioned above, this practice also takes care of the body so, in a nutshell, it is a very relaxing way of taking care of ourselves.

Besides, in fact, to make us rediscover an inner balance, meditation practice has benefits also on pathological conditions of the body, for example for cancer patients. Emotions, according to several studies , affect and influence the health of our body. and according to ancient holistic disciplines, such as Ayurveda, meditation helps to restore a state of general well-being.

Fear, anger, anxiety, negative energies can be as harmful as other common chemical toxins; these generate the so-called "stress hormones", which help many diseases to proliferate in the body.

According to Ayurveda, an ancient Indian medicine, we need to cleanse our minds and our bodies from these toxins using meditation, among other techniques.

Meditating does not mean "not thinking" or silencing the mind, but managing to find peace and serenity by examining and then fighting what lies behind our anxiety, our resentments, our unrealized fantasies. We need an internal dialogue with our ego to bring peace and serenity back to life.

Moreover, the higher our concentration, the greater is our strength, vitality, resistance to pain and fatigue. As Pranayama states, breathing care heals our body, so does the meditation that is connected to it. While meditation is practiced, the body produces positive hormones that treat us from the inside, also strengthening our immune system.

Meditation, precisely for these reasons listed so far, is suitable for all of us, since there is no need to believe in something or not to meditate. It is just a way to be happy so children, adults and older people can practice it.

Many neuro-scientists are in favour of the practice of meditation. In the East, in countries like India, China, Japan or Tibet, meditation is a part of the daily routine, as these countries have remained linked to ancient traditions and schools of meditation. Otherwise in the West meditation techniques and practices came in the sixties when the first yoga schools began to spread.

But how does meditation work? What kind of techniques can we practice? First of all, to meditate we need a calm and peaceful environment, and most of all enough time to dedicate to ourselves. In fact, meditation needs peace, so we must avoid being anxious about the commitments of the day, watching the clock continuously.

About the duration it is good to start with a few minutes and then gradually increase.

It is advisable to practice meditation at dawn and dusk, on an empty stomach, sitting with your back straight and your eyes closed or halfclosed. The position must be maintained throughout the duration of the practice so, since it will be inevitable to have numbness, especially in the legs, it is better to use a pillow or folded towel.

This is the basis of most meditation techniques, but then each involves mudra, hand positions, mantra, word to be repeated several times, and different leg positions.

The breath, as we have said, must be light and fluid, without resisting it if it increases or decreases in frequency.

Meditation techniques are many and varied, so there is the possibility of feeling confused and not knowing which one to choose at the beginning of our journey.

In the centuries, from long before the birth of Christ to today, dozens of methods have been developed in which it is easy to get lost, also because some of them are different from each other and we could rightly ask ourselves what it is the type of meditation suitable for us. For this reason we will list some of these practices, so that we can better choose which one is the most suited to our personality and to our problem or condition.

ZEN MEDITATION (ZAZEN)

Zen meditation is the classical Buddhist meditation, that has been practiced since the sixth century AD, and it is done sitting cross-legged and concentrating on one's breath, and on the present moment that we are living.

This type of meditation is used to achieve greater awareness, capacity for self-control and observation.

TRASCENDENTAL MEDITATION

Transcendental meditation is practiced through the recitation of a mantra, for example OM or another one better suited to our personality, with the eyes closed for a certain amount of time. This meditation brings harmony between us and the environment that surrounds us, giving us a sense of tranquillity and peace that pervades us every time we recite the mantra.

VIPASSANA MEDITATION

This kind of meditation draws its origins in Buddhism, and it is based on the awareness of breathing. Its practiced focusing attention on an object and on its movements, in fact Vipassana means "vision". Vipassana meditation allows us to elevate our spirit to a higher state to achieve enlightenment.

HO'OPONOPONO

This is an extremely ancient Hawaiian healing technique. It is similar to transcendental meditation since a mantra is also recited here, which however is specific. The Ho'oponopono is a practice for reconciliation and inner forgiveness.

MEDITAZIONE KUNDALINI

E'una tecnica meditativa molto complessa il cui obiettivo è risvegliare l'energia kundalini, presente alla base della nostra colonna vertebrale. Il kundalini si concentra un chakra diverso ad ogni seduta e ciò serve a risvegliare la nostra energia interiore e ad ottenere una piena realizzazione di sé.

DINAMIC MEDITATION

It is the meditation technique created by Osho and it requires movement and expression, leaving the body free to dance. The goal is to exploit movement and energy to channel the feelings that pervade us, at best.

At this point we can choose which meditation technique is more appropriate to us and deepen it, then put it into practice. These, of course, are the best known and easiest techniques to implement, but with time and practice we could increase our knowledge of meditation.

""Meditation is the only temple where, when you come in, you are really inside a temple.""

Osho

Practicing Mindfulness

"The present moment is filled with joy and happiness. If you are attentive, you will see it." – Thich Nhat Hanh

The key to soothing your immediate anxiety is to get the amygdala to calm down. It's working hard to keep your body ready for a threat, even though there isn't actually one present. One method of calming your mind is to practice mindfulness. Mindfulness for stress and anxiety calls for compassion for yourself, while developing a safe and healthy distance between yourself and the anxiety. It allows you to step back, examine your feelings, and choose how to deal with them.

What is mindfulness? You've likely heard the phrase, but may not be sure what exactly it is. Essentially it is the practice of purposefully paying attention to the present moment. It's taking a step back to view your current state as objectively and non-judgmentally as possible. Instead of listening to your amygdala's fear response, you'll tune in to your thoughts, feelings, and physical sensations. You'll learn to ground yourself in the face of stress, making your anxiety more manageable from day to day.

Mindfulness is our ability to be fully present in the moment, aware of where we are and what we're doing, without being reactive or overwhelmed. It's something that everyone can do, but consciously practicing it cultivates it into a powerful tool. Mindfulness reduces stress, enhances performance, gives valuable insights, and raises awareness.

While the idea of mindfulness is becoming more mainstream, there are still many misconceptions surrounding it. It is sometimes viewed as being mystical or something to be skeptical of, but it's just a naturally occurring awareness you're heightening. It doesn't require you to make any changes to yourself or your life.

It isn't a special skill or ability that only certain people can unlock. Anyone can do it with no prior knowledge or background. However, it does become a way of life. As you practice mindfulness, you'll find yourself noticing more of your surroundings and the things you feel. It will open your eyes to new experiences, and give you the ability to take small pauses throughout the day to recharge.

Scientifically, meditation has been shown to lower breathing, pulse rate, and blood pressure, all things that spike when anxiety is high. Extensive studies have shown that anxiety conditions are greatly reduced by practicing regular mindfulness meditation. Depressive thoughts are lower after meditation. More and more studies are being done all the time, and proving mindfulness and meditation are beneficial to body and mind.

When practicing mindfulness, you'll take control of your brain rather than letting it run on auto-pilot. The amygdala wants you to act on your fear, but instead, you're going to view it as an outsider. It can be helpful to think of yourself as the sky, and your thoughts and emotions as clouds. You can watch the clouds drift by, but the sky will always be in its place.

When learning mindful meditation, the easiest thing to focus on is your breath. When you're anxious, your breath comes faster and shallower to accommodate the fight-or-flight response. Normally, the breathing would slow and become deeper again once the threat is gone. By focusing on your breath, you'll force it into that calmer state. To start out, you can simply close your eyes and direct your attention to your breathing. Focus on slowing the breath. Let it remain natural, while gradually slowing it. This simple concentration will calm down your entire body, and help dampen that fear response that's brining anxiety.

Beyond just focusing on your breath, there are many types of meditations that you can explore. A common one for beginners is the body scan. In addition to paying attention to your breath, you'll notice and acknowledge different sensations throughout your body. It can take about thirty to forty minutes and is very relaxing.

Chapter 10 Breathing Techniques for Stopping Anxiety

Breathing is characterized as a programmed capacity of the body that is overseen by the respiratory framework and ran by the central nervous system. Breathing can be seen as a reaction of the body when it is faced with pressure, where there is a stamped change in the breathing tempo and rates.

This is a piece of the body's fight or flight system and is a piece of the body's reaction to upsetting circumstances. People have been enabled to control their breathing patterns, and studies have proven that with our capacity to control our breathing patterns we can oversee and battle pressure and other wellbeing related conditions such as depression and anxiety.

Controlled breathing when utilized in the act of yoga, tai chi and other reflection exercises, is likewise used to achieve a condition of unwinding. Controlled breathing strategies can mitigate the accompanying conditions:

• Anxiety issues

• Panic attacks

- Chronic fatigue disorder

- Asthma assaults

- Severe agony

- High pulse

- Insomnia

- Stress

Stress and Breathing

The key job of breathing is to carry oxygen into the body and expel carbon dioxide from the body through the lungs. The muscles that encompass the lungs, similar to the stomach, control the motion of the lungs, just as the muscles that are found between the ribs.

An individual who encounters stress changes their patterns of breathing. Typically, when you are on edge, you make little, shallower breaths with the utilization of your shoulder muscles, rather than with the muscles in your stomach, so as to control the breathing conduct in the lungs.

This sort of breathing intrudes on the gas ratio in the body. Then again, hyperventilation or shallow over-breathing can incredibly drag out the feeling of anxiety as it triggers the side effects of the worry to exacerbate.

The Breath-Relaxation Response

On the off chance that you are feeling unfocused or restless, you can loosen up your body by breathing gradually and tenderly through the nose to help even out your breathing patterns. Following the breathing example of a loosened-up individual can quiet the sensory system that deals with the automatic elements of the body.

Controlled breathing can likewise change the physiological condition of the individual, which incorporates, diminishing the pulse, bringing down stress hormones, diminishing lactic corrosive development in the tissues of the muscles, and managing the oxygen and carbon dioxide levels in the circulatory system.

Other physiological changes that can be influenced when you figure out how to control your breathing incorporate expanding your physical vitality and also, expanding feelings of serenity and prosperity.

Parasympathetic versus Sympathetic Nervous System

Instances of deep breathing, empower the Parasympathetic nervous system, or PNS, which is in charge of the bodily exercises when in a casual chilled out state or when you are very still. On the other hand, hyperventilation supports the inverse.

The Sympathetic Nervous System, or SNS, is in charge of the physical exercises that are identified with the fight or flight reaction in the body when stress is identified. You can look at these two frameworks like this; PNS is the quiet sister, and SNS is the insane, non-thoughtful sister that is

continuously very close to a mental meltdown.

With regards to the elements of our body, the one in particular that we can promptly control is our breathing, which is the means by which we can recuperate our bodies. By changing your breathing patterns, you can help different pieces of your body work regularly to avert the genuine reactions to stressors.

Breathing Exercises for Anxiety Reduction

There are three deep breathing activities that you can practice to help you beat depression and anxiety. As mentioned before, the action of hyperventilating can extraordinarily intensify stress and anxiety. The accompanying relaxing activities can be utilized anyplace to enable you to decrease the side effects of anxiety and stress.

Coherent Breathing

This controlled breathing activity gets you to reduce your breathing speed drastically and boosts the heart rate variability or on the other hand HRV, which is an element of the Parasympathetic Nervous System.

The strategy is straightforward and can be performed anyplace. Begin by taking a full breath in, while counting to five and after that count to five again as you breathe out. The method has you breathing at a rate of five breaths per minute.

Observe how the adjustments in your breathing influence the HRV, which is in charge of exchanging your sensory system structure the PNS to the SNS, or vice versa. What it comes down to is the higher HRV implies a more advantageous cardiovascular framework and more grounded reaction to stressors.

Resistance Breathing

Resistance breathing, as its name infers, is breathing with resistance in the progression of air all through the body. It is a way of breathing where you restricted the pathway of air or use items, such as a straw, through which inhaling and exhaling happen. A simpler method to achieve this is to inhale through your nose instead of your mouth.

Another way you can rehearse resistance breathing is by relaxing through the course of reciting or singing. This is a viable way to achieve this activity on the grounds that the vocal cords adequately thin down the air's pathway.

Breath Moving

Breath moving is the method in which you imagine yourself breathing. It causes you to inhale like you are driving oxygen to the highest point of your head and flushing out all the carbon dioxide from your body. As you are doing this, you have to envision that you are moving your breath from your lungs to the highest point of your head.

Figuring out how to control your breathing can drastically lessen your side effects of pressure and help you to defeat your anxiety disorder. Consolidating controlled breathing methods, similar to the ones recorded above, with mindfulness, can keep your mind quiet and what's more, centered around the present.

How to Control Your Thinking to Control Anxiety

On the off chance that you regularly experience odd and insane considerations that are exasperating and want to get these musings out of your head, at that point you'll be glad to realize that you can do that when you learn the most effective method to deal with your contemplations to enable you to control your anxiety.

While it isn't unexpected to have insane and bizarre contemplations from time to time, what makes it not typical and strange, is when they reoccur regularly and when you experience issues overlooking them.

These insane musings can even lead to dread in light of the fact that the thought is so irritating in nature. On the off chance that you need to have the option to deal with your considerations, you'll have to comprehend the facts that encompass these thoughts, their underlying foundations, and how to maintain a strategic distance from them.

Deal with Your Anxiety by Managing Your Thoughts

When you are encountering insane contemplations, you are encountering anxious thoughts. An individual who doesn't experience the ill effects of anxiety will experience issues understanding the different ways that anxiety can influence the body and the psyche.

The legitimate explanation to this is all individuals experience anxiety at various occasions during their life. Some normal encounters that can bring on anxiety are before a job interview, test, or asking someone out.

Be that as it may, these examples of anxiety tend to pass directly after the conclusion of the occasion. All things considered, individuals who experience anxiety disorder are entirely different from the regular anxiety others experience.

Anxiety disorder can have an effect on both the physical and emotional parts of an actual existence, which can prompt a noteworthy lopsidedness. The production of insane and terrifying thoughts is one of the essential side effects that individuals with anxiety experience and deal with.

Anxiety has the ability to change one's thinking and make you think, and accept, that you are getting out of touch with the real world. It makes you believe that you are losing your mind and, in this way, going insane.

In the event that you are experiencing these side effects, you don't have to stress over it, what's more, they are only the impacts of your anxious considerations.

How do Anxious Thoughts Begin?

There are distinctive anxious thoughts that might be considered insane. These contemplations are established in worry, however, the vast majority of them are established in the anxiety symptoms that you might be enduring.

Undesirable Images

Individuals who experience the ill effects of obsessive-compulsive disorder, OCD, are the ones that regularly experience undesirable images. These undesirable images are typically framed by their sentiments of stress, uncertainty, and the need to ensure their lives and those they care about.

Now and then these undesirable images can be activated by what they dread the most. For instance, the individuals who experience the ill effects of OCD may envision some type of serious brutality, which can be incredibly upsetting. In light of this pain, they lock the majority of the doors.

Or on the other hand, they may envision an extreme fire that may occur, so they consistently check to see if the gas is leaking. These activities are legitimately connected to their anxiety.

Unwarranted Worries

Worry is the foundation of anxiety. In this way, somebody who experiences anxiety encounters unusual stresses, which are frequently unreasonable. It makes them worry that something terrible may occur. The stressing side effect can be amazingly persistent and subjective, be that as it may, everything comes down to the anxiety sufferer getting a peculiar feeling, which makes them uneasy.

The Fear of Losing Your Mind

The genuine fear that anxiety-ridden people are going insane comes from the side effects of anxiety being so vivid to the point that they may really think they are going crazy and losing it. The particular feel of anxiety can make your head turn with numerous bothersome and fast contemplations that are amazingly difficult to control.

This fear can be irrational to the point that it influences everyday exercises and can tremendously affect the life of those with an anxiety issue.

The Most Effective Method to Avoid Anxious Thoughts

Anxiety is influenced by your thinking, and your thinking is influenced by anxiety. With one compounding on the other, the circumstance can turn out to be very difficult to control. Here are a few different ways that you can begin to maintain a strategic distance from anxious thinking and end the cycle of worrying.

See the Thought for What it is

You would prefer not to think about the certain idea because fear that accompanies it. So, you should figure out how to set your psyche not to fear the thoughts. Regardless of how insane the idea you are having is, the point at which you learn and practice to confront it, the thoughts can never again be a reason to be afraid of the thought, and it doesn't make a difference if that particular idea reoccurs.

Create the Thought Yourself

Another way that you can deal with your thoughts is by creating them before they even occur. At the point when your brain is accustomed to the thought, your fear will be stifled. The explanation for this technique is that when individuals fear something, they need to confront their feelings of trepidation and will inevitably figure out how to conquer those fears.

Put the Thoughts on Paper

One way that experts have those experiencing anxiety manage their feelings of trepidation is to record the upsetting thoughts as an approach to get it out of the head. When somebody has restless thoughts, recording those on a bit of paper resembles setting it someplace where they remain permanent, which enables the brain to unwind and not to have to worry about it further.

This routine of recording dreadful and restless thoughts tends to conciliate the psyche and enables it to overlook those thoughts in the long run. These are only a couple of the simple methods that you can start doing to manage anxious thoughts that show up arbitrarily. While you will, in any case, need to manage your fundamental anxiety, these straightforward advances can help you stop the incapacitating thoughts dead in their tracks.

Chapter 11 Towards A Worry-Free Life

Anxiety and worry are habits, which many people developed over time. The search for solutions starts when the doctor says, "disorder." However, you can avoid these conditions if you prevent it in time. So, start with the tips available in this.

5 Top Achievers' Approaches To Life

Worry leads to anxiety. If you can eliminate fear and worry in your life, you've won over anxiety. Don't waste your life worrying and miss the good things in life. Remember, the things we worry about don't always come to pass.

Emulate these simple habits and enjoy a worry-free life like top achievers.

1. Set Goals

People who live without worries set goals and focus on achieving them. By setting goals, you will have hope, vision, and direction. With these goals to guide your thoughts, plans, and steps, you can live without worry.

2. Focus On The Good

A worry-free individual think on the good sides of things, situations, people, and events. Don't feed your worry by focusing on your problems. Remember the good things and keep your mind there.

3. Take Action

Adopt the take-action nature of worry-free people. Don't put all the time into thinking, learning the steps, creating ideas but in the end, you don't implement them. Instead, decide on how to tackle a problem and act immediately.

Fear and worry can distract you. If you don't take action, you may worry about things that are not relevant to solving your challenges. And fear will set in. And the downward spiral begins.

4. Focus On Finding Solutions

Why worry about a problem when you can always look for a solution. Worry-free individuals refuse to be distracted. Instead, they focus on finding and creating solutions to their problems.

5. Take Risks

Top achievers take risks all the time. But before they do so, they need to build confidence by studying their options, weighing the odds, assessing the risks and contemplating the worst-case scenarios. Calculated risks. Calculations made, before taking risks, replace and eliminate fear and worry. So, the next time you come against an elephant, remember to eat it with small bites. Break the challenge down into manageable steps. Make a list and tackle each step, one at a time. And finally, focus on the rewards that will likely come after taking the risk.

Face The Enemy & Overcome It

Every mile begins with a single step. You can stop worrying by changing some of your behavioral tendencies that feed it. One feeling associated with anxiety is fear. Being afraid of a situation, result, event that may not occur can stagnate your life. Therefore, instead of dwelling on uncertainties and hindering your success, start inculcating these 12 good practices and habits today.

1. Learn

Uncertainty leads to fear. When you equip yourself with enough information, your problems become lighter. If you understand it, you will know how to handle it and stop being afraid. So, when in doubt, don't waste your time sweating and fretting. Instead, do the following things:

1. Do some research or Google it
2. Find the book and read it
3. Consult with someone

2. Distract Your Mind

When you are stuck, STOP! Don't overthink. Find something else to do and change the focus of your mind. For instance, you can:

1. Hit the gym and do some serious workout
2. Step out for a while and enjoy an exhilarating conversation with a friend
3. Go for that visit you've been postponing

3. Face It

Don't avoid your fears. Charge towards it and watch it disappear.

1. If you're afraid of public places, start visiting such places
2. Don't like animals? Go to the zoo sometimes or read about them
3. Take public transport if you don't like strangers

It is always better to practice with someone the first time. You can join a group or ask a friend to help you. If you try and feel like bolting, tell your companion about it. Both of you can find ways to help you get through the experience.

4. Live In The Now

Are you always worrying and afraid of the future? It's good to think about the future but not all the time. If you can help it, live your life in the now and lessen your fears of tomorrow. Make a conscious effort and try out the following activities:

1. Notice the sound of the shower
2. Watch the movement of rainfall
3. Perceive the freshness of the morning
4. Don't think about dinner in the morning.
5. Discover the different tastes of coffee

6. Notice what other people are doing

7. Listen to what your colleagues are saying

8. Wait until Monday to tackle the job you have in the office.

9. Participate in the things happening around you.

10. Bills, bills, and more bills. Don't allow these thoughts to make you anxious. Create a plan on how to pay them and follow it.

5. Postpone The Worry

Don't give it any time at all. Once worrying wants to interfere with your daily activities, stop it immediately. Remove them from your mind and note them down on your worry list for a designated worry time.

6. Discuss It

Talking to someone can help you to let go of worry. The right person can provide the insight you need to solve your problems. You can meet with your closest friends for simple issues. However, when the object of your worry grows beyond what they can handle, get professional advice.

7. Reduce Your Computer Habits

A computer screen can increase anxiety. Yes, that includes your handphones and tablets. If your social interactions center on the Internet, you may be spending more time than healthy watching the screens. Another thing to reduce is your social media time. Please, cut it down and eliminate unnecessary comparisons, regrets, and desires that make you anxious.

8. Exercise Is the Key

Decrease your worries faster by exercising your body. Exercise is good for the body, yes, but it also helps the mind to relax. You may be surprised that exercise works better than prescription drugs when it comes to reducing anxiety. You can dance, do Yoga or play tennis. Dancing lifts your spirit, yoga brings calm to your mind, and playing tennis takes your mind off your worries.

9. Meditate

Meditation helps to decrease worry. If you've not formed the habit yet, start it today and watch the difference it will make. There are many different schools of meditation. Do some research and find the nearest or most convenient meditation centers or schools and sign yourself up for a short course!

10. Aromatherapy Helps

Studies have shown that scents can alleviate worry and stress. Once you perceive the scent of some essential oils, it helps you to feel lighter. For instance, researchers have discovered that grapefruit scent can reduce worry so, try it out next time and feel better.

11. Change Your Way Of Thinking

Life can't be perfect, so accept it and ignore the reasons for worrying unnecessarily. Also, life is very unpredictable. If you start feeling low that your plans didn't work, anxiety will creep in. Therefore, change those unhealthy thought patterns.

12. Eat Healthily

Eat to maintain a functional body system. Lean on energy giving foods. Anxiety can leave you weak. Therefore, eat when the body needs it. Stock your kitchen with all your favorite foods at all times. If you can't cook sometimes, eat out or have them deliver it to you. You need your blood sugar to be normal, and your body system functional at all times.

Don't spend time worrying about a problem or situation when you can spend lesser time solving it. So, if you must overcome anxiety, start now to overcome fear and worry.

Chapter 12 The secrets for increasing productivity while reducing stress

What is your Stress Marker? On a scale of 1 –10 with 1 being deeply relaxed and 10 being stressed to the max where are your right now?_______________

Have you ever wondered why some people seem to get more done in a day than most and experience less stress? A big part of the answer is that these people have learned organizational and productivity skills. To provide you with the productivity habits of highly effective managers I had the pleasure of interviewing one of the best people on the subject, Lee Ann Kleinfelter an efficiency and productivity consultant. Lee Ann has shown hundreds of executives and business owners how to get more done in less time through better planning/prioritizing, effective decision making, managing work flow, and making the most efficient use of their skills and time. As you will see this was a great interview full of productivity tips and clear action steps.

HV: Lee Ann, as you often mention, the very first thing that people need to do to be more productive and experience less stress is to define their goals. What are the keys to having successful goals?

LAK: The first thing is writing them down – they need to have your commitment to be implemented. You need to ask yourself what do you want to get out of your time – what do you want to get accomplished? Until you clearly articulate this to yourself and to others, you are following a trail without a map. Whether setting goals for your year, quarter, week or your day – you need to identify what is important for you to spend your time on. Time management doesn't work unless you know what your goals are.

"You need to ask yourself what do you want to get out of your time – what do you want to get accomplished?"

HV: So, identifying what is most important is a major step. What are other important steps for goal setting?

LK: Setting aside time yearly, quarterly, monthly, regularly and consistently to set goals and review them. Where are you going? Identify what is working and what isn't? There is nothing wrong with modifying your goals - change happens. If you don't articulate your goals, they will never happen. Many people don't think about setting aside the time to do this, but you do have to schedule the time. What helps is to have a place where you can think without being interrupted; a room or a getaway place away from the office, where you can be undisturbed.

HV: Any other tips for goal setting?

LAK: Start with the most important goals and with a small number; say, five things you want to achieve. As you achieve them you can add more to your list. If you start with too many, you will overwhelm yourself and nothing will be done well.

HV: What are some common goals you hear from clients?

LAK: Financial goals, number of employees that are being served, reaching a certain level of certification, personal education and educating their staff. Getting their business to the next level. What kind of vacation they are planning. How they are developing their spirituality. I encourage you to have goals in all aspects of your life so you can have a map of where you are going.

HV: What are some common productivity goals?

LAK: Some examples are minimizing paper work by being more electronic or getting off junk mailing lists. Others include learning to delegate so you can do more of what you do best or developing a calendar to block out times to work on your strategic plan. The bottom line is that people want to get more things done during the work day so when they go home, they are really "home" and not stressing about what didn't get done.

HV: Prioritizing and goal setting go hand in hand. You just mentioned using a calendar and identifying important tasks. What are some good ways to prioritize work?

LAK: We need to prioritize and shuffle our tasks on a daily basis. Once a day it is a good idea to check what is on your list. For some people early morning works best, for others it is the end of the day. You have to look at the entire list of work and see what has been done, what still needs to be done and what new information has come in. Pick 3-5 goals for any given day. Your top goals should relate to revenue generation (customer service, product design, doing the service of the company) and the value expected of you. The second level goals are two steps away from revenue (conferences, meetings, proposals, collaboration). The next level of goals to complete is three steps away from revenue (paperwork, reading, updating files, administration duties). If nothing else gets done – at least your top 3-5 have been finished. When you complete these then you can go onto other things.

"We need to prioritize and shuffle our tasks on a daily basis."

Another problem that people have in setting goals is that they select a goal that is a huge task – like creating a marketing plan. There is no way that you can do this all at once. It is best to break this down into smaller steps, with each step being about one hour long.

People tend to think that interruptions get in the way of their priorities – it really needs to be the other way around. You have to allow priorities to be priorities and not allow yourself to be interrupted. A great way to work with this is to have certain times of the day when you are uninterruptible and certain times of the day when you are. This means not answering the phone, avoid checking emails and closing the door if need be for certain periods of time throughout the day. In this way you can focus on your priorities and get them finished.

HV: Any more tips regarding this?

LAK: Yes! Write your goals down; prioritize them electronically as well as on paper. Using both media reinforces that you will remember them and stay focused on them. Have action files that hold the top 3-5 things to do today. The more we can train ourselves to focus working on these, and the more we can visualize them being finished, the more likely we are to complete them.

HV: That's so true! We have been talking about writing things down, which brings to mind the question: Is it helpful to have "to do" or "action" lists?

LAK: These lists only work when they are all together in one place. When you have several lists then it doesn't work. If you have lists in different places with different things on them then it is very difficult to prioritize and delegate your time. There is no need to have a list for personal things that is separate from a list for work priorities. It is all you! It's your 24 hrs. – your time. If need be, you can separate the page or use different colors but have it all in one place. This is the key to making lists useful.

A lot of people like to carry this info around in their smart phone -which is great. You also have to make sure that you have a system that can be easily updated and captures information from all the sources that you receive information.

HV: How important is it to include small unimportant things on your list as well as the bigger – more important things.

LAK: This is a great question. Both are really important to put on your list because it is important to clear your brain. I have a client who takes a walk in the morning or spends the morning just writing and part of that writing is to come up with the "to-do" lists and then prioritize them. Clearing your mind is a good thing and in my experience most people don't do enough of it because they feel they don't have enough time. When information is running around in your head you are working harder because you are trying to remember what to do – it produces more stress and less efficiency. Your list is a great physical reminder of what needs to be done, instead of trying to remember it all in your mind. Be sure to include the small and large tasks, just prioritize what's most critical to get done.

HV: How do you deal with procrastination?

LAK: Procrastination is putting off making a decision. Keep in mind that there is healthy procrastination and unhealthy procrastination. Healthy procrastination occurs when you put off doing something that someone else can do for you. For example, when there is filing to be done and you let it pile up or information needs to be entered into your data base. This is healthy procrastination because someone whose time costs less than yours can do this work.

"Keep in mind that there is healthy procrastination and unhealthy procrastination."

An example of unhealthy procrastination is the piles and piles of paper that sit on your desk with no action plan or method for dealing with it. Handle it once and deal with it. We need to teach to ourselves that any decision is a good decision. When you are on the fence, nothing moves forward. I like to handle procrastination by getting someone else to help me, and taking lots of small breaks when I'm working on something I don't like doing.

HV: Can you say a little more about making decisions?

LAK: When you know that you have a decision that is difficult, put it on your "to do" list and meet with a friend, family member, colleague or boss that can help make a decision – someone who can help guide you through your indecisiveness. Those are the times that you need help and when you get it, you will get things done. This is the power in working with others. A lot of business owners and executives often think they have to make all decisions on their own, which of course is a fallacy. Another great way to get help is by joining a mastermind group where others can assist you in making decisions.

HV: Lee Ann, I have heard you talk about the value of grouping like activities or "pocketing" as you call it. Can you describe what this is and why it is helpful for being productive?

LAK: Statistically we perform better and are more efficient when we put like things together. For example if you are going to file, have everything that needs to be filed set out and focus on the task of filing. If you are going to make phone calls, group all the phone calls you need to make, and then plan a specific time to focus solely on these. It is proven that on average, when you get interrupted, it takes 15 minutes to get back to what you were doing. If you are interrupted 10 times in a day imagine how much time you are no longer efficient. It helps to have like tasks together. Identify like activities and then schedule time on your calendar to work with these items.

"Statistically we perform better and are more efficient when we put like things together."

HV: A big challenge for a lot of people is delegating – would you address this?

LAK: Delegating is a hard thing for many people because they don't want to give up control or are fearful something is not going to be done exactly the way they might do it. The reality is that when you start to delegate you will be so relieved because someone else is doing the filing, or entering names into a data base, or keeping your calendar. This frees up your time and energy to get to higher level work. How much is your time worth?

HV: What is the best way to find someone to assist you?

LAK: The best way is just start telling everyone you know that you are looking for an assistant, for someone to do "XYZ." You might also consider a virtual assistant – someone who works for you remotely from their computer. It is not necessary to have someone in your office. Many tasks can easily be performed virtually. At home, ask yourself what can your children do, is there a neighbor or a stay-at-home mom that would like a few hours of work each week? Be creative and ask away!

HV: How important is sorting information to being productive? Are there good ways to do this?

LAK: Yes! An important step in being productive is to have a system in place for processing information when it comes into your home or office. For example – what happens when business cards come into your office? Are they given to an assistant to process? Shipped to a virtual assistant to file? What happens next? You need a streamlined process for handling this. Another example of utilizing a system is how you sort mail. Once you sort mail it either needs to get filed, tossed, or put into an action folder which is part of your daily tasks. Having systems in place makes an office work efficiently and effectively. If there is no system then chaos ensues and the condition of your office gets worse and worse. You want to set up systems to deal with regular tasks. Remember from our discussion earlier that it is best to sort tasks by placing like things together.

HV: Is there a good way to calendar action items?

LAK: Most people find it easy to do things like scheduling bill paying because there is a due date. The same strategy can be used for getting administrative tasks completed. You can schedule one day a week or every couple weeks two days a week or a certain time of day to work on administrative tasks. Calendar your action items according to their priority in getting them done today, this week, or this month. When they are calendared you have knowledge of what's on your schedule so you can make informed decisions to other tasks that appear.

HV: Are there any particular programs or tools for scheduling that you recommend?

LAK: There are many programs for calendaring available. A few good options include Google Calendars, which I often have a husband and wife share because the calendar is on a server (a web hosted site). Most smart phones have functions for calendaring as well, which can interface with your computer and Outlook or Entourage email software programs. Day Timer and Franklin Covey also have electronic versions of their paper copies that you can integrate with Outlook. Both paper and electronic systems work. The important thing is to have a system. Whatever you do, make sure you have only one calendar, otherwise you will be double booking!

HV: What about tips for setting up your office at home or work for making it more efficient and productive?

LAK: Sometimes setting up an office for efficiency requires a third party. Having some else's eyes can be really helpful because we often get in our own way. We are so used to how our office works and how it doesn't. So whether it is a friend or professional, have them take a look at your office. How can you can make the best use of your space for where you sit, where you store supplies, where you need to have your equipment? Remember you need room for your computer, printer, phone, calendar, and room to spread out. I find that many people have desks that are too small which prevents them from spreading out. You also want to have your desk facing the door which will give you more light, energy and see people coming and going for better Feng Shui. Avoid having your desk in a dark corner of the room.

You also need to think about the flow of information as it comes into your office. Where are you going to put the mail when it comes in, whose going to sort it, how will it get put into your action folders and where do they go?

Make sure that you have enough book shelves or storage space – most people don't.

Labeling drawers, files and supply materials can also be helpful. If you are expanding your business, hiring an assistant, or have others use your office, labeling will make it easy for others to find their way around your office.

Look for ways to automate and at the very least find methods to streamline your efforts. For example: Are you paying your bills by hand or are you paying them on line? For any given task, which steps can be eliminated or made more efficient? Can you do something quicker or easier?

"For any given task, which steps can be eliminated or made more efficient?"

Review your space at least once a year. See what is working and what can be improved upon.

HV: Are the any products that you recommend for organizing your office and enhancing productivity?

LAK: Products I like to recommend include clear see-through folders – sometimes called project folders. In addition to protecting and organizing information these folders let you see through them and you instantly know what is inside of them. Bookends are another item that I often suggest as well as book shelves. If you like to keep your files on top of your desk or credenza instead of in a file drawer, then metal file dividers work well. Be sure to make sure they are big enough to hold 8 ½ by 11 files. When things are flat they take up more space and are hard to find. Getting materials and files vertical makes them easier to find and use. In and out bins only work when you are in an environment where there is somebody putting in stuff and someone taking out on a regular basis. For most small business owners that work by themselves, there is no one doing this. If you do work by yourself then you do need to have a box for sorting incoming mail and area for action files, but there is no need for in and out boxes.

Another good tool is space to hold all the products that your printer uses such as labels, checks, paper, printing cartridges, etc. A storage unit that fits underneath your printer works well for this. Be sure to get one that has drawers which can hold all the products that you use with your printers.

HAV: Do you have any tips regarding filing?

LAK: We use 20% of the papers we have in our files, 80% we never touch. So in both deciding what goes into file as well as cleaning them – be ruthless – do you really need it? Here are three questions I suggest you ask yourself regarding what goes into your files:

1. "Does my life or business depend on this paper/document?" If so you have to keep it.

2. "Can I get it somewhere else?" For example can you pull it off the internet?

3. "Will I use this document in the next six months?

Another helpful idea for dealing with files is to consider archiving and cleaning out both your paper files and electronic files once a year. Many people find the time between Christmas and New Year's perfect for this as business is usually slower then. If you don't clear your files they will get bigger and bigger, and quite cumbersome to use. Why go through all that stuff? Just make a decision from the beginning. Do you need it or can it be tossed out?

"If you don't clear your files they will get bigger and bigger, and quite cumbersome to use."

HAV: What about clutter?

LAK: When we are surround by clutter we don't have the space to think clearly, perform well, and be at our best. The more things that are surrounding you the less focused you will be because you are distracted. Minimize what is on your desk – set it aside, get it off your desk and then put a date on your calendar to deal with it or throw it out if it is not serving you. Some people are afraid to get rid of things. Generally, this is an unfounded fear that's based on old beliefs. Do you really need that file full of vacation brochures from ten years ago? Probably not! If you do have something of value – is it something you really need or would someone else find it more useful? Ask yourself which things can you give away, donate to others, or simply throw out?

Action Steps

1. Setting up your office for efficient work flow & to maximize productivity

2. Scheduling a friendly office visit and critique

1. Setting up your office for efficient work flow and to maximize productivity.

As we have in this , one of the keys to maximize productivity is to have an efficient office environment. An hour or two of organizing now can save you many hours of frustration, stress and dramatically improve office efficiency. Schedule some time on your calendar now and follow the exercise below based on the acronym SPACE. "S" stands for sorting. "P" stands for purge – to get rid of. "A" means to assign a space for the things you keep. "C" stands for containerize – to put in containers. "E" means equalize or maintain the system you have set up.

S=Sort: Sort or group like things together such as files, office supplies, electronic equipment, user's manuals, etc.

P=Purge: Throw out or give away whatever you don't need or use. This process goes hand-in-hand with sorting.

A=Assign: Assign a place to the things your keeping: Once you have put like things together where will you put them: In a file, a cabinet, on a credenza, in a closet, or on your desk?

C= Containerize: Once you have decided where you are going to put items you grouped together what kind of container will you put them in? In drawers, on shelves, in bins or boxes, in your desk, on in a file folder?

E=Equalize: Maintaining the system. Most people know how to set up a system but maintaining the system is where people often get tripped up. The easy way to deal with this is to calendar time to maintain your system. Schedule 15 minutes or more once or twice a week to keep your system organized and working for you.

2. A friendly office visit and critique.

Ask a friend or colleague to visit your office and have them comment on the following:

____Size and placement of desk?

____ Placement of computer and printer?

____Placement of phone and other equipment?

____Do you have enough shelf space?

____Does anything need to be labeled?

____How well does your filing system work?

____Is there any clutter?

____Anything else they can think of that would make your office space more efficient or enjoyable to work in?

Chapter 13 How Cognitive Behavioral Therapy Helps Treat PTSD

Most people who experience traumatic events usually have a difficult time adjusting and moving on with their lives—but eventually, they manage to adapt and carry on. However, if the debilitating anxieties and flashbacks carry on for months or years, you certainly have the condition known as post-traumatic stress disorder (PTSD).

Symptoms of PTSD

The symptoms of post-traumatic stress disorder might show up as early as a month within the traumatic event, but in some instances, the symptoms can wait for years. Post-traumatic stress disorder hinders you from living a normal life and causes significant problems especially on your social life, work life, and relationships. The following are the four categories of PTSD symptoms:

- Intrusive remembrances

- Avoidance

- Negative changes in thoughts

- Altered physical and emotional reactions

Intrusive Remembrances

If you had healed from a traumatic event, your mind wouldn't go back to reliving the horrible experience. However, for someone with PTSD, their mind tries to get them to relive the horrible experience in a myriad of ways. The affected person starts experiencing vivid flashbacks, which obviously ruin their mental stability. They may also start experiencing nightmares on a frequent basis, and these nightmares are related to the horrific event. Additionally, the person experiences severe distress when they run into things that are associated with the traumatic event. For instance, if a young woman was raped at night, she may get seriously distressed every time she passes through the exact spot she had been raped, calling to mind the horrible details.

Avoidance

It's human nature to want to avoid confronting things that have traumatized you, but then a well-adjusted person shouldn't have any difficulty revisiting their past when there's an incentive. A person afflicted with PTSD totally avoids speaking about their traumatic past. In fact, they might not take it kindly if someone approaches them wanting to find out about their trauma. They will also go to great lengths to avoid people, things or situations that are associated with the horrific event, considering that these things could trigger nasty memories.

Negative Changes in Thoughts

Sufferers of PTSD develop negative thought patterns about themselves or the world. For instance, they may consider themselves as worthless, develop an inferiority complex, and develop a deep-seated hatred against the entire world. They see the world as being against them. They also tend to become hopeless and it discourages them from making any bold steps since they don't believe they can achieve anything. Their memory becomes stunted, especially concerning various aspects of the traumatic event. Since they hate the world, they have extreme difficulties starting and maintaining relationships, and alienate themselves from those that care about them, for instance, friends and family. They lose interest in activities that they once enjoyed and also have a hard time feeling positive emotions.

Altered Physical and Emotional Reactions

After you have gone through a traumatic event, you might become a little more cautious and sensitive, but that tendency eventually goes away as you adjust.

However, when your reflexes continue to be amazingly active so that you are easily startled or frightened, it is indicative of PTSD. People with PTSD seem to be always expecting danger, and this makes them appear extremely cautious, especially in public settings. They may also start to engage in self-destructive behaviors, such as excessive drinking, excessive sex, and other addictions, which are mere attempts to drown their pain. They tend to have difficulties first getting asleep, and then having quality sleep. Sufferers of PTSD have a hard time focusing on the task at hand as they become easily distracted by external stimuli. They tend to give exaggerated emotional and physical responses, giving them an appearance of emotional instability. Additionally, they experience intense feelings of shame and guilt, as they might blame themselves for the traumatic event. For instance, it is not uncommon for a woman who was raped to feel guilty and blame herself for making herself ripe for the ordeal.

Causes of PTSD

Considering that research into mental health conditions is still at the early stage, there's no concrete evidence to point to the real cause of PTSD. But conventional knowledge indicates that distressing and traumatic events are largely behind PTSD.

- Painful events: you don't have to through them yourself. Even witnessing a painful event is enough to cause your PTSD. For instance, if you witnessed the loss of your loved one through a degenerative disease.

- Family affair: if your parents have had various mental illnesses, you are at risk of developing these illnesses yourself, and you might pass on this condition to your progeny as well.

- Environment: if you associate with people who have symptoms of PTSD, you may eventually ape their traits that eventually birth PTSD in you.

- Brain problems: if there's a disconnect between how your brain processes external stimuli and the responses it gives, it may result in chemical and hormone imbalances, resulting in PTSD.

Risk Factors

Almost anyone can develop post-traumatic stress disorder, but the following factors increase your probability of acquiring this illness.

- Lack of a support system: bad things happen all the time, but they shouldn't hold us hostage. If you have a good support system, you should get over the trauma and go back to being normal. However, if you have no support system, you might get crushed under the intense emotions and develop PTSD.

- Childhood abuse: for instance, being brought up by ruthless parents or getting sexually abused.

- Sensitive job: taking up a job that exposes you to the dark side of human life. For instance, military, police photographers, and surgeons.

- Mental health: if you are already battling other mental illnesses, you are more likely to develop PTSD.

- Unhealthy habits: you are also likely to develop PTSD if you have taken to unhealthy habits such as excessive drinking and binge eating.

Treating Post-Traumatic Stress Disorder (PTSD) with CBT

identifying the symptoms

This initial step is critical because apart from helping a therapist understand the unique aspects of the illness bedeviling their patient. It is also a perfect time for them to bond, considering that the success of cognitive behavioral therapy depends on the collaboration between the therapist and the patient. The following are some of the questions that the therapist will ask in order to have a better understanding of their patient's troubles:

- What runs through their mind when they remember a tragic event?

- What are their physical reactions for remembering a traumatic event?

- Do they experience invasive memories of the traumatic event?

- Do they experience nightmares related to certain traumatic events?

- To what extent have they lost interest in things they once enjoyed?

- How detached are you from other people?

- What activities, feelings, and thoughts have you been avoided since the trauma?

- Do you have any difficulty remembering any aspect about the trauma?

During this phase, the therapist expounds on what ails the patient and tries to make them understand how the trauma influences various aspects of their lives, and the actionable steps they may have to take in order to restore their lives to normalcy.

They must also set achievable goals. The goals should guide the patient back into a normal life where they are not affected by their traumatic past. The goals should be as specific as possible:

- Stop blaming myself or my spouse for the accident

- Start playing ping pong again

- Start embracing the people of the world instead of shunning them

- Start going out more

- Not run away from any reminders of the accident

explaining the rationale of treatment

At this stage, the therapist is done selling the patient to CBT as the best treatment approach, but they may want to expound on how the treatment works. The therapist gets to explain how CBT addresses the deep-seated factors that influence PTSD and highlight types of people who are susceptible to this illness.

- Flexibility: the thing about CBT is that it is not rooted in some rigid set of rules. It is virtually a technique of self-exploration, except you have someone to watch over you and ensure that you don't falter. In order to come up with the most effective treatment, both the therapist and the patient must work together.

- Attitude: CBT not only cures you of your mental illness but helps a lot in terms of improving your attitude toward yourself and others. Studies show that a person's attitude is every bit as important as a person's qualifications for career advancement.

- Goal-setting: CBT allows you to have a multiple-thronged approach to your issues. You can achieve many goals by adhering to particular exercises.

understanding how your trauma caused PTSD

Some of the traumatic events that can lead to PTSD include:

- Fatal road accidents

- Sexual assault

- Mugging

- Miscarriage

- Domestic abuse

- Sexual abuse

- Witnessing violent deaths

- Terrorist attack victim

- Being taken as a hostage

- Floods

- Degenerative diseases

When we experience trauma, the last thing on our mind is political correctness or critical thinking.

We can easily grab an incomplete thought and run with it. CBT helps us be objective so that we may have a clear idea of how the past affects our present conditions.

If besides experiencing something traumatic you had also been suffering from depression and anxiety, you are in a much greater risk to develop full-blown PTSD.

The therapist helps you understand that PTSD comes about due to the following reasons:

- Survival mechanism: one school of thought says that PTSD is merely a biological response aimed at strengthening your survival capacity. For instance, the flashbacks are merely attempted by the brain to get a clear glimpse of the details of the horrible event so that next time you are more than prepared to prevent a repeat of the same. The feeling of being on edge is aimed at sharpening your reflexes.

- High adrenaline: when we are in stressful situations, the body secretes adrenaline to trigger quick action. Some people might not lose the ability to produce high levels of adrenaline and it could lead to PTSD.

- Brain changes: if you have undergone significant brain changes, you may be unable to process external stimuli accurately, leading to false emotional responses, and eventually PTSD.

developing positive thoughts

Once you learn of the various ways your mind is relying on inaccurate data to arrive at decisions, you can purpose to restructure your thoughts and eradicate PTSD.

- Cognitive restructuring: as a victim of a traumatic event, you might have become so shocked that you want nothing that reminds you of that experience. But that's the wrong approach. You should welcome the idea of being able to revisit your traumatic past and even talk about it. Once you demystify the trauma you can move on quite easily.

- Play the script to the end: once you have undergone something traumatic, your body might make you feel on edge. This is a biological response aimed at making you more aware of your environment. Thus, you might find yourself scared of getting into certain areas or situations. In such instances, you ought to play the script to the end, so that you will find out nothing terrible will happen anyway.

- Muscle relaxation: once the anxieties and fears build up inside of your mind, you can engage in progressive muscle relaxation in order to relieve yourself of these negative energies.

therapy progress

As you keep practicing the exercises your therapist has assigned you, you will experience positive results. At this stage, you must start pushing the limits so that you may quicken your recovery.

Chapter 14 Working with Emotions

By now, you have a clear understanding of why and how emotions impact your life. But how can you turn negative emotions into more positive experiences? While negative emotions can be uncomfortable, you do not need to allow this discomfort to affect your life. You may not have control over the emotions you experience, but you do have control over how you react and work through these negative experiences. This will reveal how you can better utilize your emotions to improve your life.

Understanding emotions

Being emotionally healthy refers to your ability to not only understand your emotions, but also the thoughts and triggers than cause certain emotions to occur. When you are an emotionally healthy person, you are able to deal with stress in a more proactive way, bounce back more easily from negative events, have stronger relations, and enjoy a happier life, overall.

Being emotionally healthy involves you being able to express your emotions appropriately, find balance in life, be grateful for what you have, be resilient, actively participate in mind and body calming activities, and take better care of yourself. An emotionally healthy individual has taken the time to fully develop their emotions, understand how to process them, and recognizes when they are covering emotions so they can better cope and resolve emotional responses.

Emotional development

Emotional development is a process start starts from birth. From a young age, you learn the proper ways — or what you know to be the proper ways — to express your emotions. You learn to understand these emotions by recognizing them in others, as well as in yourself. Unfortunately, while this is something we learn at a young age, it is often not something that is properly taught or thoroughly addressed when we are young. Often, we never understand or even question why we react to certain emotions as we do, as it is just an automatic reaction. For many positive emotions, this is of little concern, but the way we react, and process negative emotions can have serious consequences.

It is not until we are older that we even begin to question whether we are appropriately expressing our emotions or begin to realize we may not have a clear understanding of what emotions we are experiencing.

Through continuous emotional development, we can better understand our own emotions. We can learn why we experience emotions, as well as how we express these emotions and, through this, can better read emotions in others.

Emotional processing

Emotional processing refers to how well you are able to not only handle stress and other negative emotions or events, but how easily you are able to move past them. When it comes to emotional processing, many individuals lack the skills that will allow them to bounce back from setbacks or effectively use their negative emotions in a more positive way. When one does not understand their own emotional process, this can often result in developing anxiety disorders, being affected by stress more easily and frequently, and increase the risk of falling into a depressive state. Not being able to properly process your emotions leads you to constantly relive the experience. When you begin to dwell on the experience, you are unable to move on and learn from it. Your emotional process system directly reflects how high your emotional intelligence is.

Covering emotions

Covering emotions is a process we tend to partake in to remove the intense emotional response that follows an emotional experience. This is typically done with negative emotions so we can feel instant relief from the discomfort these feelings can cause. While this can be effective in the short term, in the long term, leaving these emotions unresolved can lead to a number of unwanted and inappropriate behaviors.

We cover emotions by labeling them as other emotions or by doing something that will give us instant gratification, like eating chocolate when we feel sad or angry. Understanding what we do to cover our emotions is the first step to understanding how our emotions affect our behavior and is vital for gaining control over these emotions.

What must also be understood is how many negative emotions arise in response to other challenging emotions such as hurt, embarrassment, fear, and disappointment. When you understand the true source of where your emotions are coming from, you can begin to uncover the real emotion you are experiencing but trying to hide from. For example, anger is a strong negative emotion that can cause us to act irrationally and unkind to ourselves and others. But, often, our emotional response to anger is actually a way to mask what we may truly be experiencing. Anger can often cover:

- Hurt

- Resentment

- Disappointment

- Shame

- Guilt

- Fear

Before reacting to an emotion, it is best to pause and look at the whole picture. Could the intense feeling actually be hiding a deeper, unresolved emotion that needs to be addressed?

Why and how emotions can motivate and help you move forward in life

It is easy to feel motivated when you feel good, so it's natural that you would want to do more to ensure that you maintain those positive emotions. But the true challenge and struggle is working through the negative emotions that can knock you back and keep you stuck.

Negative emotions are labeled negative simply because of the uncomfortable way we tend to feel when we experience them. This, however, does not mean negative emotions have to be viewed as a bad experience.

Wanting to experience more positive emotions is not a bad thing, but if you do not learn how to handle the negative emotions you will never be able to fully enjoy the positive ones. Negative emotions can give you a better understanding of who you are, what you value, what is important in your life, and what can push you to achieve all the goals you set in your life.

There are a few things you need to understand about negative emotions in order to use them to motivate as opposed to hold you back.

1. Negative emotions can help point out things in your life that need to be changed or addressed. Negative emotions are warning signs. They send you signals that there is something that you are not resolving in your life. When we feel negative emotions, it can often be due to the fact that we are struggling internally over being dissatisfied in a certain area of our life. For instance, feeling constant anger, anxiety,

or sadness about your job is a clear indication that something about your career needs to change. Maybe it is time to ask for a raise? Or maybe you are ignoring the fact that your work does not align with your purpose? By really looking at where these negative emotions are coming from, you can identify the true reason they keep occurring and you can then take the appropriate steps to improve this area of your life.

2. It is actually not healthy to maintain an upbeat and positive persona. While negative emotions can be difficult, constantly faking or acting as though negative emotions do not affect you can be exhausting. When you embrace the fact that negative emotions, just like positive emotions, are a natural and healthy occurrence, you can learn to use them to push past your setbacks and get out of your comfort zone. It is when we try to suppress our negative emotions and act as if they do not exist that we see the most negative effects on our mental health because of them.

3. Negative feelings like shame or embarrassment can be used to motivate you

to learn and improve on skills you may be lacking. Instead of dwelling on these emotions and the negative response you have because of them, use the opportunity to push yourself to improve. This will then allow you to avoid feeling the negative emotion in the same situation again, as well as using these emotions as a motivator to try again and do better.

Negative emotions can also help build resilience. When you learn to properly address negative emotions and understand how they can benefit you, you learn to use them to develop your resilience. Having resilience means you are able to push past setbacks, to work through difficulties, and find solutions when you are confronted with an obstacle. Resilience is necessary for living a healthy and successful life. Most people lack the emotional resilience to overcome adversities simply because they become stuck and consumed by the uncomfortable reactions, they have to negative emotions.

Building emotional resilience involves developing seven key characteristics:

1. Emotional awareness. Your ability to recognize and identify what you are feeling and why. Emotional awareness also relates to your ability to understand other people's emotions.

2. Action-oriented. Being action-oriented, means you persevere toward goals and trust yourself and the steps you are taking to achieve these goals.

3. You are in control. Instead of turning to outside factors to define or to make things happen, you take responsibility for your life. You understand that you have control over your own actions, and no one has the power to make you feel inadequate, less than, or unworthy — unless you give them this power.

4. Optimistic. Building emotional resilience requires being able to see the positive in every situation. Emotionally resilient people know there is a lesson in every encounter, and look at problems with an open and positive mindset.

5. Supportive. Emotional resilient individuals provide plenty of support to others and surround themselves with people who are also incredibly supportive.

6. Can laugh at obstacles. Instead of being thrown off when problems arise, they can look at each setback with a playful attitude. They understand that laughter is the best medicine in stressful situations and find humor in situations that would most likely defeat others.

7. They shift their perspective. Instead of ignoring their mistakes, they address them head-on. Emotionally resilient people know that when they make a mistake, it is the best opportunity to learn and grow. Through every challenge they face, they look at the situation from various perspectives to gain the most information as they can to come up with the best solution. This allows them to take effective action and find meaning in all they face.

How to increase your emotional resilience

1. Regularly engage in positive self-talk. Resilient individuals know their strengths and

understand what they are capable of. This is why they are able to handle and persevere through many of life's challenges. Continuously thinking of yourself in a negative manner will only create actions that mirror this image you have in your head. When you begin to focus on shifting your internal dialogue to a more positive one, you will begin to obtain more emotional resilience because you will begin to truly believe in what you're capable of.

2. Increase your awareness. Begin to keep track of your emotions. Gaining a deeper understanding of your own emotions and why they occur results in you being able to understand the emotions of others. It is only through building your self-awareness that you will learn how you react to difficult situations and how you can begin to react in a more positive and effective way.

3. Build up your support system. When you surround yourself with supportive individuals, you will eventually begin to take on these supportive characteristics. Having the right support system in place can help you face

more challenging obstacles, and you will not feel like you are battling these challenges alone.

4. Make physical activity a daily occurrence. Being emotionally resilience also involves understanding that your health can be negatively impacted by negative emotions. As we have in great length already, negative emotions can severely damage your physical health. To better ensure these emotions only affect you in the most positive ways, it's a good idea to make exercising a daily habit.

5. Find your spiritual side. Those who feel as though they have a greater purpose in life tend to be more resilient. Being spiritual does not necessarily mean you have to attend services or look at organized religions; spirituality can relate to a number of different practices. Essentially, it means you feel a deeper connection to nature, others, and yourself.

Do not want to die young? Live today!

Never rummage in the past and do not regret the decisions made and the actions committed. Then you stop worrying about what cannot be changed and, therefore, turn your attention to the concerns of today.

In addition to the decisions made, circumstances that you cannot argue with can affect every person's life: health, appearance and ability, in other words, potential and heredity. Each person comes to this world with a certain genetic combination, which cannot be changed by anyone. Therefore, it makes no sense to worry about this.

Do not be sad about the past. Past evils are powerless, they can no longer harm you. You will stop worrying as soon as you forget yesterday's insults and defeats. Do not aggravate the wounds, do not remember what can't be returned. Do not frighten yourself with the ghosts of future troubles - only one future, and you can imagine an endless amount of misfortunes, most of which will never happen.

Trouble. Willingness number 1

Waiting for trouble does not diminish disappointment from failures when they happen. The American psychologists came to this conclusion after conducting a series of experiments with students. Most people believe that if you mentally prepare for the worst — for example, failure in an exam or defeat in a competition — then it will be much easier to endure these troubles if they really happen. However, this view is refuted by an experiment conducted by psychologists from the Pacific University of Seattle and the University of Washington.

Unexpectedly, it turned out that the students, who from the very beginning did not believe in a positive result, felt worse than those who were confident of success, but overestimated their strength. But in those cases where the result was good, the degree of positive emotions was approximately equal, according to the journal Nature.

Researchers believe that a person's response to failure is mainly determined by his general attitude towards life, and not by the degree of preparedness for certain circumstances. It turned out that the old advice "to be prepared for the worst" simply does not work, and the pessimistic attitude makes a person a loser. Those who are confident of success, even in case of failure, are convinced that they acted as a whole not so bad.

If you are experiencing a breakdown, if the problems you face seems insoluble, heavy, even overwhelming, use the following exercise, which consists of two stages.

Exercise: Release your desires!

The first stage - Choose a time so that you don't need to rush. If you don't find an interval between cases, make yourself a day off - forget about duties or reassign them to someone. Do not refuse this event only because you cannot allocate time for it, unless, of course, you need to replenish your own forces. So, select the time, ask others not to disturb you, you can turn off the phone and go to bed.

The second phase - Promise yourself to suppress any attempts to start doing something. Lie still, holding back even eye movement. Keep track of emerging goals that require your execution (from the slightest desire to turn in bed on the other side to the need to do some urgent business or think through some projects). Relax as much as possible, immerse yourself in the present, chase any predictions and watch from the sidelines. If the desire to take some action will still appear, and this will certainly happen, "release" your wishes to the will without your own support. Become an indifferent witness of their impulses, look at them from the side, from the position of the third, as something not interesting and completely distant to you. If necessary, strengthen yourself with the thought that you need to gain strength and the only way to achieve this is not to expend them. You also should not think that "here I am now having a rest and will be engaged in what now comes to my mind." You, on the contrary, are obliged to let go of your desires, allow them to do what they want (wander), but without your participation.

Today, we constantly worry about past failures and mistakes and also worry about the future. In addition, because of laziness, we often postpone for "later" what should be done now. And in doing so, we do not pay attention to what is most important - the moment in time.

Full immersion in hope and anxiety leads to a loss of energy and, ultimately, to failure. But the person who gradually, step by step, does what he should do, he achieves the success of his own accord. Fortune herself turns to face him.

It is important to be able to distinguish whether you are planning something for the future, or just worry about it, you should spend every moment of this time only with benefits. The more you think about troubles, the more suffering there will be when you experience them. It treats possible events impartially.

Conditioning your mind to live in the present tense

You can only worry if you are mentally living in the future of which you are dreaming or afraid, or in the past where something has happened that you have been experiencing so far. If you live in the present, you will not be able to worry. For example, are you worried at the moment? Of course, no! This is because you are reading this book, and your concentration relieves anxiety. A person cannot think about two things at the same time.

You overcome fear and anxiety if you live for today, and even better for the present moment. Just make a statement that "you will soon...!" Express a positive statement and stick to it for a certain period of time. Do not think about the future that will come later, and your worries will disappear.

Exercise: Coordination of activities in areas of life today

1. Define in detail every area of your life.

2. Describe in detail what you have in each area. This does not mean "wife," "work."

3. Then determine what you are doing in each area. Not what you should do, but what you really would do today.

4. Take the first item in the list of "Coordination of Activities." Find out in each area that you want to put in the first paragraph. That is, determine the starting intention for each area. Then take the next item, "Desired Goals," and determine what is located here for each sphere. Do this for all items in the "Coordination of Activities" list for all areas.

5. Prefer the most interesting field. Carefully work through the structure of this area throughout the list, until it is agreed.

6. Fully analyze the remaining areas throughout the list until complete agreement.

7. Pay attention to any contradictions between the spheres and deal with them.

Thus, in the events, there is nothing absolute: good or bad. To achieve the goal, it is necessary to make serious efforts. And even if you end up with defeat, it can be put at the heart of your future success. But if you are concerned in advance, afraid to make a mistake or lose, then you will fail. We can act only here and now. And because of the anxiety, this present moment is wasted.

Conclusion

By this point, you have learned that you do not have to be a prisoner to your anxiety. While not every type of anxiety can easily be solved, it is essential to remember that you are currently running a marathon and not a race. The life changes that you can make using this information and worksheets will forever change your life if you allow it. It is never easy for a person to change their lifestyle or to accept things that are hard in life, but this book gives you the tools to succeed.

Every person's body is different, just like every mind is different. This book is full of strategies for all different kinds of people. Just because one exercise doesn't work for you; it doesn't mean that there isn't one out there that will help calm you or help your anxiety. Trial and error are the game until you find what is right for you. The most important thing is not to give up. You are worth living a life with less anxiety.

This workbook is meant to be your companion. The more you practice it, the better your life will become dealing with your anxiety. Anxiety is not something that has to run your life instead of you. Anxiety should be something you learn to simply acknowledge as a dinner guest and move on without fear that it will start a food fight. That is why it is important to practice the skills you have learned in this workbook daily. Write down your feelings daily. This is a day to day attack on anxiety in the fight for your freedom from it.

You have learned what anxiety orders look like and what their symptoms are. There are questionnaires in this book that can help you get an idea of what type of anxiety you might be experiencing. Keep in mind there is a multitude of mental illnesses out there, and yours may not be included in this workbook. Your doctor will have the best diagnosis for you.

Mindfulness, meditation, and breathing exercises are a good way to combat your anxiety. Remember that when using these, the sole purpose is to clear your mind and allow the feelings to come and go without judging them. It is okay to acknowledge your anxiety because it is as real as you are. Other therapies that might be of some use to you are cognitive-behavioral therapies. This is learning to approach the anxiety and defeating it through facing it.

Your lifestyle plays a significant role in your mental health. Simply changing your diet and exercise routine can have a large impact on how you feel on a daily basis.

It is okay for you to start out with small changes and work up to the bigger ones. Taking on a ketogenic-type diet is a large undertaking, but with dedication and willpower, you can make the changes you need to make for your anxiety.

Not all medicinal options have to be pharmaceutical; however, before taking any supplements, it is best to contact your healthcare provider. There are a lot of naturalists out there who can help you with any interaction questions you may have, as well. Self-medicating your anxiety is not an option.

The important thing to remember is that you can feel "normal" again. The advances being made in anxiety studies are showing the promise of people living full and happy lives that are not overrun by anxiety disorders. Not every disorder has a cure, but there are definite steps being made to help deal with them so that they are not a factor in daily life.

www.ingramcontent.com/pod-product-compliance
Lightning Source LLC
Chambersburg PA
CBHW070700250726
48662CB00001B/210